# THE HEYDAYS

## The Story of
## Ernie Teal
## as told to
## Margaret Garbett

HUTTON PRESS
1992

Published by the Hutton Press Ltd.
130 Canada Drive, Cherry Burton, Beverley,
East Yorkshire HU17 7SB.

Typeset and printed by
Image Colourprint Ltd.
Anlaby, Hull.

ISBN 1 872167 38 1

*For Doris and Peter,*
*with our love.*

*A donation will be given to Cancer Research,*
*the principal beneficiary of the Walkington Victorian Hayride,*
*for every copy of this book which is sold,*
*in loving memory of relatives and friends who have died*
*and in the hope that it will help others to live.*

# CONTENTS

# ACKNOWLEDGEMENTS

I would like to thank Charles and Dae Brook of Hutton Press for their confidence in my abilities; John Markham for advice so freely given about the buildings of Beverley and for all the information culled from his book 'The Friary Families'; Barbara English for advice and encouragement; the staff of Beverley Reference Library for their friendly efficiency and interest; the Hull Daily Mail for the photograph of Ernie and Doris used on the cover of this book; the entire Teal family for their collective memory; my brother and sister-in-law, Geoff and Carole Shaw of the Poldark Mine in Cornwall for peace and quiet interrupted only by lovely meals while I scribbled furiously to meet deadlines; and finally Doris and Peter, our respective spouses, for their patience and encouragement during the last eighteen months. Doris has gently corrected facts and toned down the more colourful stories while supplying us with gallons of tea and wonderful home-made cakes. Peter has uncomplainingly chauffeured me around and translated my scribbles into type, correcting spellings and grammar and curbing my excess of hyphens as he did so.

Without their unstinting support this book would not have been possible. We love them both dearly.

M.G.

# FOREWORD

My involvement with Ernie has been long and rewarding. We differ in our memories of where we first met. My version is that it was when I was holding a meaningful conversation with a Hayride horse on Beverley Westwood in the company of that year's Chairman of the Hayride Jim Latham, at that time News Editor of BBC Radio Humberside. Whenever, it has been through my broadcasting career with Radio Humberside that our friendship has flourished.

It was in the Spring of 1991 while recording our regular monthly 'Countryside' feature for the weekend breakfast shows that the idea for this book was born. Our recording sessions were invariably just a preliminary to a fascinating hour or two for myself and my husband Peter as we thawed out after our forays into the winter countryside and were plied with tea and home-made cakes by Doris.

We had long admired the village of Walkington, always receiving the warmest of welcomes as we attended its many functions or walked its many footpaths. I bombarded Ernie with questions about the people we met, the buildings, the customs, the pond and the origins of the Hayride as it approached its Silver Jubilee. Peter was fascinated by his stories of the war and we both listened eagerly to tales of his Beverley childhood.

On that day in March when we arrived home and I unpacked the mere eight minutes of tape I had recorded it all seemed such a waste. Somebody, I said, should write it all down. And so I have.

Many people will have heard some of these stories. Very few people have heard them all, not even members of the immediate Teal family. This is not my book. I am merely the spinning wheel gathering together the many strands and spinning them into the threads with which to weave the fabric of the lives of Ernie and Doris Teal. It is their story, told as far as possible in their words. Time and hindsight can distort memory and the view of the war is necessarily as seen through the eyes of a serving soldier rather than a politician or a historian, but to the best of our ability it is all true.

If we have offended anyone either by omission or inclusion we apologise and will hope to rectify it publicly in the next book! In the meantime I hope you find the following account of the long and happy life of this remarkable couple as fascinating as I have.

Margaret Garbett
Anlaby Park and Walkington, April 1992.

# PREFACE

With more than my allotted span of three score years and ten tucked under my belt I have so very much to be thankful for. Each day that dawns is still exciting and generally filled with happiness.

To whom do I owe thanks for this long and wonderful life? First of all to God of course. Then to my Mother and Father who brought me into this world and gave me the best they could of everything in hard and trying times.

To my beloved Doris to whom I owe more than I could ever possibly repay. Her love and steadfast loyalty throughout the years have never faltered and she is more precious to me than gold.

To our family who are so good to us and who we love so very dearly and especially to our grandchildren who bring us boundless joy.

To our village of Walkington and the priceless fraternity of every-loyal friends and supporters who helped to make all our ventures so successful. If only Anno Domini could have been held at bay we would have gone on from strength to strength but golden memories of what we all achieved together will never fade.

To my close neighbours with whom we have shared the joys and sorrows of the passing years, carrying out to the best of our ability that most important commandment 'Love thy neighbour as thyself'.

Without the devotion and unselfishness of Margaret and Peter Garbett this book would never have been, and I thank them for everything from the bottom of my heart.

Ernie Teal
Walkington, April 1992.

# Chapter 1

## IN THE BEGINNING

George Ernest Teal MBE was born on November 1st 1919 in a mews cottage off North Bar Within in Beverley in the East Riding of Yorkshire. It was only a stone's throw from North Bar itself, a pair of massive wooden gates set in an archway, all that remains of the walls which surrounded the town in the Middle Ages. Today the shop fronting the cottages and stables is almost as famous as the Bar, being the home of Burgess' Ice-cream.

Almost immediately after his birth the family moved to a tiny mediaeval house crouched in the shadow of Beverley Minster which owned the property. It had formerly been occupied by 'Uncle Tom Dalby', a relative of the family who was a fruiterer and who, having prospered, was able to move to better accommodation.

The product of the uniting in marriage of two East Riding families Ernie is immensely proud of his Yorkshire roots and is fiercely patriotic. Although he is known as Ernie or Tealy to his thousands of friends and admirers his wife Doris calls him George, a name he shares with his late father and grandfather. His great-grandfather, James Teal, was a blacksmith at Holme-on-the-Wolds, six miles north of Beverley, and that is where his father, George Frederick Teal, was brought up after he was orphaned soon after his birth in 1897.

Ernie's grandfather, George Teal, was a groom at Denton Park Hall, just outside Ilkley in West Yorkshire. He had gone to collect a new hunter from Otley a few miles away but on the way back it threw him, rolled on him and killed him. The locals 'reckoned he was kettled up', but drunk or not his death devastated his young wife who followed him to the grave within six months leaving their baby son homeless and destitute. He was taken in by his father's brother Herbert and his wife to be brought up with their two sons in the smithy at Holme where they all lived with grandfather James.

In 1914 seventeen-year-old George Frederick and his two cousins went to war. Sadly both the cousins were killed but although badly wounded and reported missing George did survive and in 1917 returned to Holme having been honourably discharged on medical grounds. His name can be seen on the village Roll of Honour. His broken-hearted aunt never got over the loss of her two sons and in 1918 George left the smithy and moved to Beverley where he met and soon after married Alice Railton.

Within a short time Alice was pregnant. Returning servicemen were offered a pension for life or a lump sum and George Frederick, having given up the security of the family home and a career in blacksmithing and with the prospect of three mouths to feed, chose the lump sum of one hundred and fifty pounds. In later life during periods of unemployment he was to regret his decision as comrades-in-arms who had chosen the pension at least had a steady if small income. Although looking back Ernie realises that they must at times have been grindingly poor, as a child he was never aware of it. He puts it down to having 'a real good mother'.

Ernie's maternal grandmother, Hannah Maria Railton, lived at 9, Norton Street, a cul-de-sac off Grayburn Lane near Beverley Westwood. It was there with his beloved Granny Railton that young Ernie was to spend a good deal of time. She came from Cranswick, a village between Beverley and Driffield and only about five miles from Holme-on-the-Wolds. There were more relations at Harpham, about half-way between Driffield and Bridlington. It was through visiting these families that Ernie acquired his love of the countryside which in later years was not only to dominate his life but to bring him so much into the public eye.

Before he went into the army Ernie's father had worked on farms as well as helping in the smithy but in 1919 he had to take any work he could get. What jobs there were were mostly in the building trade and he was taken on as a bricklayers' labourer by Tarrants who had been given the contract by Hull City Council to build the North Hull Estate. He was earning two pounds a week but with unemployment rising even further the Council decreed that only residents of Hull could be employed on the project so he lost that job.

At least the family had a roof over its head. They had been able to rent number 6, Highgate, one of a pair of 15th century timbered houses owned by the Minster. At one time most of Beverley consisted of timbered houses but very few remain. The Highgate houses were demolished in the 1950's and replaced by modern apartments and no proper record of their construction or embellishments survives. What is known is that they had brick infilling, not wattle and daub, that they had carved traceried window heads and a carved and moulded cornice between the ground floor and the jettied first floor. There was also a blocked three-light window again with a traceried head and a crown-post roof. Ernie remembers it as 'damp, dark and full of blackclocks', (cockroaches). By the time Ernie and Doris moved in after the second world war it had been renovated and had electricity installed but in the 1920's it must have been a nightmare to keep clean, dry and warm, especially during periods of unemployment.

One thing the Teal family were rarely short of was food. As well as Alice Teal's good management there was the added bonus of 'free' food from the countryside around Beverley. George Frederick was country bred and 'useful with a 4.10' and Ernie remembers the dairy at number 6 being filled with pheasants and rabbits. In the desperate 20's with so many people in the same boat neighbours helped each other. A butcher called Arthur Jebson who had a shop in the town used to have a stall in the Saturday Market. When it got to about eight o'clock in the evening he would auction off his remaining produce and you could buy 'a load of stewing meat' for threepence or fourpence. Ernie's Dad blamed Winston Churchill for the depression because he took Britain off the Gold Standard.

Life was often even harder in the villages than in the towns. There was no money in farming - there were farms to be had for no rent at all but nobody wanted them. Many children died from diseases associated with poor housing, inadequate clothing and malnutritiion and there were no modern drugs to treat them. Pneumonia, diptheria, TB, rickets and scarlet fever were rife. It was said that you could tell by looking at the children which ones had fathers who were in work - or good at poaching!

Despite the Teal family's well stocked larder one of Ernie's earliest recollections is of sitting in a darkened room with a tiny coffin which his mother was decorating with little balls of cotton wool. His Dad came in and picked up the coffin and took

9

it away. His mother was too ill to go to the funeral of her baby son, Ernie's brother Raymond, who had died of pneumonia when he was only three weeks old. His death was blamed on the mid-wife who said what the sick baby needed was plenty of fresh air and flung open the windows. It was mid-winter and Florrie Tomlinson, a family friend, remarked on how cold the baby felt, but even she didn't realise that he was dying. (Florrie's husband Lot later died and she re-married to become Mrs Duffil.) It was she who accompanied George Teal on his sad journey in Billy Camm's hansom cab to Queensgate cemetery with baby Raymond. Later Ernie's other brother, Len, spent time in the TB Hospital at Raywell but Ernie seems to have escaped relatively lightly apart from his bowed legs which have grieved him in later life.

There were always plenty of friends and neighbours to rally round in times of grief and hardship and the area around the Minster had its fair share of 'characters'. 'Norfolk Jack' (who came from Norfolk!) lived in the corner house of Highgate near the Minster. On Sundays he used to walk about in a 'claumer' coat and green trousers. ('Claumer - claw-hammer - swallowtail.') The chimney of his house was always blocked by jackdaws' nests so his front door was left permanently open to let out the smoke from his fire.

The Dolly Maine brothers, one of whom was both deaf and dumb, were window-cleaners. Then there was 'Cornet Solo' who used to practise his cornet every Sunday afternoon and spoil everybody's after-dinner nap.

Charlie Lucas ran a barber's shop in Highgate and as Ernie remembers 'had a bald head and was a rum 'un'. The local lads could earn a copper or two on Wednesdays (cattle-market days) by holding the horses and ponies of visiting farmers while they went inside for a hair-cut. They could earn a penny, twopence or sometimes even threepence a time. Wednesdays were also characterised by the big heap of 'oss-muck' outside the shop. On one occasion Ernie himself went into the shop for a hair-cut. His mates assembled outside the window and laughed at him. Ernie started to laugh as well and Charlie Lucas, having cut half his hair, turned him out and told him not to come back until he could behave himself.

Milk was delivered by Frank Fussey on his bicycle. He was still pedalling when he was seventy-five and by then his back was permanently bent with leaning over the handlebars. Many people couldn't pay when the weekly reckoning came, but Frank never resorted to what was rumoured to be the old custom of collecting debts. The story went that if a woman didn't have enough money for the bill she would shout 'Whoa' to the milkman's horse from her bedroom window! Others had a different way of making up the deficit - they used to top up their milk-churns from the nearest pump.

Ernie remembers always having plenty of bread, milk, eggs and sausages, 'good sausages, not like today. No fancy stuff in them, just meat in a skin'. Doris says he is very difficult to please with modern sausages, comparing them all unfavourably with the ones of his childhood. The Teals also had a roast joint on Sundays, unlike some families who rarely had meat at all. Everyone was caught up in the same poverty trap, shop-keepers and customers alike. As soon as the men got their wages or dole money it had to be handed straight over to pay off their debts. There were no income support schemes, family allowances, social security or rent and rates rebates. If you had no money you went hungry, even the dole was only paid for a limited time

*The House in Highgate, Beverley, right foreground.*

*George Ernest Teal winning a baby show!  (1920).*

and rigid means tests were applied. Officials visited the house and decided which family possessions could be sold to raise money. If schoolchildren had no shoes a ticket could be obtained and taken into Reynold's shop to get some boots 'on the knock' - that is on credit. But they still had to be paid for. Ernie remembers wearing heavy boots from a very early age. They always caught on his ankles and skinned them raw.

Because of his mother's illness after the death of her baby son (she had rheumatic fever) Ernie went to live with his Granny Railton for long periods when he was still quite small. Her house in Norton Street was only a few hundred yards from the Westwood, where she used to take her young grandson 'sticking' two or three times a week. As they collected twigs for kindling she taught him about the flowers and the birds, about the trees, the seasons and the weather and instilled into him his abiding love and knowledge of nature's lore. She stored the bags of kindling under the stairs and it was she who got up first in the mornings to get the fire going and boil the kettle for the early morning tea.

"It wasn't like today," remembers Ernie. "Women were the ones who did all the household chores and always stayed at home and looked after the children." It was hard, often heavy and dirty work, with no labour-saving devices, but his abiding memory is of how clean and fresh his mother always looked by the time his father came home, however hard she had worked during the day. She always changed her clothes and put on a clean pinafore and had a hot meal ready for him.

Granny Railton would sometimes take young Ernie with her into Wright's shop on the corner of Westwood Road and even on occasions buy him a few sweets. When he got a bit older he exploited this by going in with his cousin Clive and saying, "Ice cream apiece and me Granny will pay at weekend." Old Mr. Wright ran the shop until his recent death at the age of 98.

Only rarely was Ernie taken to see his father's family at Holme-on-the-Wolds. More frequently he and his mother and grandmother would visit his granny's cousin Anna, whose husband was a gamekeeper at Harpham. They would travel by train from Beverley to Lowthorpe, then walk to Harpham, birthplace of St. John of Beverley and noted for its primroses, still one of Ernie's favourite flowers.

Christmas was a quiet family festival, and however short of money they were there was always an apple and an orange and a few toys in Ernie's stocking. One year he got a little flashlight, and remembers trying it out in the cupboard under the stairs. As he got older there was great competition among his schoolpals as to who had the most powerful torch, the ambition being to own one that would shine as far as the Minster clock.

It was some time after the death of baby Raymond before Alice Teal recovered her health and produced more children. Muriel is two years younger than Ernie, and Len and Margaret much younger still. They all still live in the area - the two sisters in Beverley and Len at Lund, not far from Holme. The children took their historic home very much for granted, disregarding the fact that it was one of the oldest houses in Beverley. They disliked the "blackclocks" which filled their shoes every morning if they had been unwise enough to leave them on the floor. (It was said that they were attracted by the flour and water paste used for wallpapering.) At least they had a flush toilet, although it was outside, and their own cold-water tap. Most of the other houses shared the pump and a row of earth closets in the communal yard.

Highgate is still cobbled, and still has its breathtaking view of the Minster which towers over the houses, but in today's climate of sympathetic conservation the Teal family's historic home would not have been pulled down so unceremoniously. It would have been restored and kept as a unique record of a way of life long gone.

## Chapter 2

## WILLINGLY TO SCHOOL

When he was five years old Ernie started school at Minster Moorgate Infants, transferring a couple of years later to Minster Boys School, only a hundred yards or so from his Highgate home. The headmaster was George "Dodie" Whitehead and although a strict disciplinarian he is still revered by Ernie as a 'helluva good fella.' As a boy he worshipped him and had great respect and affection for the other teachers who were there at the time - 'Minchy' Moore, Horace Maston, Dicky Wynne, Maggie Downing and Maggie Sugden are some of the ones he remembers.

All the teachers were held in awe and every classroom had its bent, battered and well-used cane. Ernie was no angel and several times was chastised by his class teachers for relatively minor misdemeanours such as not working hard or making a mess of his writing. On one memorable occasion his crime was more serious. Long Lane, quite near to the Minster, was a mecca for lovers of wild-life with its dykes and ponds, copses and meadows. There you could find waterhens, 'peggy whitethroats', flycatchers and, in their season, tadpoles, frogs and dragonflies.

One spring day Ernie and his friend Jack 'Battny' Willison decided to play twag and spend the afternoon birdsnesting - a favourite pastime. Next morning their class teacher, Charlie Coward, asked them for their absence notes from their parents. They confessed they didn't have any, and they were sent to the Headmaster. He took them in front of the whole school, pushing back the screens between the classrooms so that everyone was assembled together and before laying them over a stool and giving them twelve strokes each with his personal cane he lectured them on the folly of truancy and vowed that he would make sure that they would never dare to transgress again. When Ernie got home he was still feeling very sorry for himself and sniffling miserably. When his father arrived home he asked him what was the matter. "Nowt", answered Ernie. "When I ask you a question the answer is never 'Nowt!' " thundered his father. "Now - what's the matter?" "Dodie Whitehead laid me ower," confessed Ernie, "because I played twag," whereupon his dad gave him another good hiding, telling him he'd brought shame on the family and adding, "When I send you to school it isn't to play twag, it's to get some knowledge into that skull of yours so that you'll be better off than me when you're my age."

Despite - or maybe because of - the strict regime Ernie loved school, if not for entirely academic reasons. He was keen on running and entered enthusiastically into sports days. He was even keener on football and so, fortunately, was his headmaster. It was considered a great honour to be picked for the school team and to be able to wear the school jersey. Football practices were held in Baxter's Field on Hall Garth Farm, close to the school, to the south of the Minster. The farm, alas, is no more, it has given way to a modern housing estate, but in the 1920's and 30's Ernie remembers it as 'a good old spot'. He tried his hardest to get into the team, practising in his spare time whenever he could get hold of a ball, but he was twelve before he finally achieved the coveted honour and then it was partly by chance.

One Saturday morning he was walking down Highgate bouncing a football when he encountered his Headmaster, who asked him where he was going. "Just for a kick about," said Ernie. "No you're not - you're coming with us. We're off to Hull - Leslie Drewery's not turned up - you're in the team." Ernie remembers every detail of his youthful debut as right half against Brunswick Avenue 'B'. At that time Southcoates Lane and Blundell Street were the top teams in Hull. Ernie's mother was as thrilled as he was about his success and cut the account of the game out of the Sports Mail. It mentioned that a new boy had arrived on the scene by the name of Ernest Teal and that he had played well. After that he never looked back, regularly representing the school with such great players as Jack Porter, Eric Blizzard, right winger Raymond Tyler, Charlie Perry, Billy Scott, Frank Acaster and Jim Gibson. Sadly most of them were killed in the Second World War.

Eventually Ernie achieved the greatest honour of his young life when he played for Beverley Boys against Hull City Boys, winning 1 - 0. Beverley Boys used to play on Watts' field in Pig Hill Lane now, to Ernie's disapproval, renamed Manor Road. Often there were two to three thousand spectators, as boys from all the surrounding villages were involved. At half-time there was no score and Dodie Whitehead told Ernie's Dad that it was largely due to his son. "It's Ernest that's stopping them. The left wing is an International Schoolboy player but Ernie's at him like a terrier. He just can't function." Two days later he called all the school together for what would have been Ernie's proudest moment, as he announced that just one boy from the Beverley team had been chosen to play for Hull and District and that boy was Ernest Teal. Unfortunately Ernie was at home with tonsillitis and missed his moment of glory.

Fortunately he recovered in time for the match, which was away to York City Boys. His Dad was by that time working at Beverley Shipyard and took a day off without pay to go and see him play. York were a good team and he ran up and down the touchline shouting encouragement to his son, but to no avail. Ernie, probably overawed by the occasion, lacked what he called "oomph" and at half-time he was replaced by a substitute. He was disappointed for his father who had gone to considerable expense to watch him play, but he had enjoyed his day and he continued to enjoy his football. If he had been good enough he would have liked to have been a professional and would have played for Arsenal - or England - 'for nowt.' He doesn't agree with the huge salaries earned by today's players when they represent their country - he thinks the honour should be enough. He admits that this is an old-fashioned view, but contends that many of his friends felt the same way and that they would have sold their souls to play for their country.

One 'perk' that he and his friends appreciated was the glamorous image it gave them. When they turned out on the field in their white shirts, kept clean and sparkling by mother and granny, they drew admiring glances from the girls. All the parents used to turn up to watch and if they were picked for the 'big match' they thought of little else for weeks. They used to play against the other Beverley teams - Spencer Boys, St. John's Boys and the top team, St. Mary's - and against Tickton and Walkington in the Hospital Cup. Ernie remembers opponents such as Bob and Willie Tomlinson from Admiral Walker's Estate, the Richardsons, Clive Pape and Barnes from the King's Head Pub - all good players. There was no 'bashing, spitting or crippling one another, no rotten fouling.' Mr. Whitehead saw to that. "He would have taken the skin off your backside if you'd fouled like they do today," says Ernie.

Apart from football most of Ernie's free time was spent in the surrounding countryside with various groups of schoolfriends. Birdnesting was a continuing preoccupation - not something he condones now, but a universal pastime in his young days. On one occasion he had gone with three friends, Battny Willison, Bunny Ribey and Eddy Ewen, to a plantation in Dogkennel Lane on the way to Bishop Burton. There was a pond there as well with a waterhen's nest from which they took several eggs. Then a 'stoggie' flew out of a tree and Ernie climbed up to investigate. There were two eggs and he shouted triumphantly to his pals, "Got them." But they shouted back to the hapless Ernie that "Gibbie" was coming. P.C. Gibson of Bishop Burton and Walkington waged constant war on the trespassing lads of Beverley and wasn't going to miss out on the opportunity of catching one of them red-handed. Ten-year-old Ernie clung to the trunk of the tree hoping not to be noticed, forgetting that his faithful terrier was sitting at the bottom gazing patiently upwards. Gibbie joined the little dog, sitting down and getting out his pipe. He didn't look up, merely remarked "The longer you stay up there the bigger hiding you'll get. You'll have to come down some time so it might as well be now." Eventually Ernie reluctantly descended to receive his punishment and run off home after his friends. As a postscript to that adventure, when he was on leave during the war he went into the Telegraph pub dressed in his army sergeant's uniform and saw P.C. Gibson in civilian clothing. "Remember me?" he asked him. "Would you like to try it now?" P.C. Gibson very sensibly chose an alternative solution and bought him a pint.

Another favourite spot for birdnesting was "Union Bushes" on Beverley Westwood, behind what is now the Westwood Hospital, but which was then the "Union" building, or workhouse, where bed and board could be had in exchange for a day's work and at Christmas hard-pressed families could go for Christmas dinner. There was an Orphanage there as well, and Ernie and his friends used to look with pity on the children in their ugly uniforms. Union Bushes was also known as "First Bushes" as they were the first ones you came to as you entered the Westwood from the Beverley end. It was there that Ernie climbed up a tree to investigate a crow's nest. Unfortunately it was occupied by the female carrion crow and as he put his hand over the edge it jabbed its beak into his nose. He bears the scar to this day.

Wherever they went the boys were on the look-out for the "slops" as they called the police and would run for their lives to avoid being clouted with a rolled-up cape. Even worse was being reported to their parents. They had great respect for the keepers of the law, if not for the law itself.

Another favourite occupation in Union Bushes was 'mousing'. Most of the boys had or could borrow a terrier. Ernie had a whippet cross called Jugger which was an excellent mouser, although now he thinks the creatures they caught were actually voles. With Peter Thompson and Frank Windle they would block the voles' runs among the tree roots then send the dogs into the beds of nettles to catch them. They used to spend hours and hours this way when they were eight or nine years old and kill thousands of voles. Again Ernie looks back with horror at the cruelty of it, but then it was part of life, as was harvest-time, when they would wait in the fields as the cutter went round and round leaving a smaller and smaller area of standing corn. Finally the rabbits would have to run and boys and dogs ran after them. If you could take home three or four couple you'd be sure of a warm welcome.

The Westwood was a paradise for children with all manner of innocent pastimes, most of them free. But if they had a copper or two they could wander across to Black

*Mr. G. Whitehead, Headmaster,*
*Minster Boys School, taken in 1949.*

*Schoolboy Ernie.*

*Back row, left to right: Gordon Bell, Jack Porter, Len Hunter,*
*S. Harrison, Billy Scott.*
*Second row, left to right: Horace Duggleby, Ron Gillyon, Eric Blizzard,*
*Frank Acaster, Ernie Teal.*
*Front row, left to right: Chuck Forest, H. Bugg, Charlie Perry,*
*Les Drewery, Ken Granger.*

Mill, where Charlie Hutton dispensed lemonade for twopence with a ride on the swingboats included in the price. All the gate-keepers at the entrances to the Westwood also sold lemonade and 'goodies'. One way of earning the money to pay for these treats was to stand by one of the ponds which then abounded on the Westwood and wait for golf balls to be hit in. Then they would roll up their trousers, wade in and stand on the ball till the golfer appeared, when they sometimes got twopence or threepence for their pains.

Toys as such were practically unknown, but home-made bows and arrows were part of their games of Cowboys and Indians in Burton Bushes, another of the copses on the Westwood. Generations of young Beverlonians spent whole summers out on this tract of grassland, still used by thousands today.

When it was too wet or dark to venture far from home whips and tops or "winda-brekkers" would be brought out into the street, and hoops for bowling. The boys banded themselves into gangs and the inevitable fights took place, but on the whole there was less violence and much less crime on the streets than there is today. Mostly it was harmless mischief.

There were of course seasonal treats, such as the Saturday each year when Hull Fair visited Beverley just for one night - always eagerly anticipated. On November 5th a huge bonfire would have been built in Moody's Field in Highgate. Once Ernie remembers picking up a firework which he thought had gone out, but which was in fact still smouldering. He thought it had blown his hand off but luckily he suffered no permanent damage. At Christmas as well as carol singing there was 'Lucky-bodding'. The 'Lucky Birds' went out first thing on Christmas morning knocking on the doors of the big houses in New Walk and wishing the householders a Merry Christmas. If they *were* lucky they would get a 'tanner'. The Reverend Wigfall lived in North Bar Without. He was the parson at the Minster and always seemed to have plenty of money, so he was invariably good for sixpence.

Some of these extra funds could be spent at the 'pictures' on a Saturday afternoon. It cost twopence to get in at the Marble Arch in Butcher Row where there was a doorman known as Blind Wilson because he had only one eye. It was all one price and Ernie and his friends favoured the balcony. They would take catapults and a supply of little green apples or tiny 'taties' for 'kelting' the unfortunate audience seated below. If they were caught they were immediately thrown out. If they had to sit downstairs and their view was blocked by a big lad they would direct their catapults at him in the hope that he would yell out, whereupon Blind Wilson would 'bray him and chuck him out.'

At the end of the performance they would sometimes leave by the back door and walk down Tindall Alley, one of the roughest areas of the town. The householders would stand on their doorsteps and if you weren't careful you'd get a clout as you walked by.

There were other picture-houses, but they didn't have a Saturday matinee. The Playhouse in Saturday Market (the old Corn Exchange) was owned by Mr. Simmonds, a great benefactor to the town who Ernie remembers as a kind and generous fellow. On cold days when there was a weekday matinee and he had sold as many seats as he thought he could he would come outside and invite the unemployed men standing round the square to sit in the front row and keep warm.

The Regal wasn't built until the mid-30's when Ernie was about sixteen and it's doubtful if he and his friends would have been able to afford it even then, although it was supposedly free of the fleas and even the occasional rat with which the older establishments were infested.

The boys' favourite films were Westerns, especially Roy Rogers, which they used to act out afterwards on their beloved Westwood, rounding up the hapless cows into a herd and then stampeding them. If caught they would get into 'a helluva row.' As far as Ernie is concerned there's only ever been one 'real' Tarzan - Johnny Weismuller. Compared with him all the others have been 'whimps'! 'Tarzan' was a favourite game in Burton Bushes. Frankenstein on the other hand frightened them to death. Once, after watching a particularly terrifying episode Ernie jumped on his bike and pedalled like mad for home down the middle of the dark street. He forgot about the posts put to stop cars and ran straight into them, doing far more damage to himself and his bike than any monster would have done.

Despite the poverty and hardship of the recession-hit 20's and 30's Ernie had an extremely happy childhood, and he is eternally grateful to his parents for making it so. It sowed in him the seeds of determination and self-sufficiency which were to see him through many a crisis in later life and, as he says, he was never bored. There was plenty to do and life was full of fun.

## Chapter 3

## DIB-DIB-DIB

Apart from school the most important influence on Ernie's young life was join-ing the Scouts. He readily admits that he was 'a bit of a tear-away', always willing to join in any projected mischief, such as birdnesting, enticing pigeons from their lofts or chasing the banty hens kept by many of their neighbours. Understandably this wasn't a popular pastime as far as the grownups were concerned. At that time the Curate of the Minster was SWEJ - the Reverend S.W.E. Jones and with his assistant Stanley Bell he ran the 4th Beverley Minster Scouts. Mr. Bell came from Molescroft at the Northern end of Beverley and his father had a shop in the town centre. Ernie had already decided that 'galloping about the streets and getting into mischief' wasn't really a good thing, and was easily persuaded to join the troop.

They met once a week in 'Charlie Johnson's Carriers' - a big buildng in Keldgate which had a conveniently empty loft. SWEJ owned three powerful BSA air-rifles and under close supervision he would take the troop to the rifle-range and there teach them to shoot. Ernie can still remember the instruction drilled into them. 'Get the tip of the foresight in the centre of the backsight - - - - -.' The discipline was strict, the standards high and stood Ernie in good stead for the rest of his life. None of them realised of course that within a few years they all would be shooting in a very different climate as they fought in the war to end all wars. Many of them never came back but Ernie was one of the lucky ones and maintains that many a time the skills he learned in the Scouts plus his country upbringing enabled him to survive when others died.

Every summer the troop travelled to Scalby Beck just outside Scarborough for their annual camp. They paid twopence or threepence a week throughout the year towards the cost, a considerable effort on the part of many of the families during those hard times. If they hadn't saved enough the Reverend Jones and Mr. Stanley Bell used to go round dropping money through letterboxes to make up the difference without embarrassing the parents. The boys and their equipment were taken to the camp by Charlie Johnson in his big lorry plus three or four cars, a real luxury in the 30's. When they arrived all the gear had to be taken across the beck by way of the stepping stones as there was no vehicular access to the camp-site. Charlie used to carry the huge scout-trunk by himself. He was, says Ernie, a big strong fellow! They all used to line up in awe to watch his precarious journey across the swift-running beck.

Once unpacked and the tents erected the lads revelled in the freedom of being away from home and out from under the watchful eyes of parents. They each had ten shillings to spend, an enormous sum in those days. Mostly it went in the first two days on the delights offered by Scarborough, but within the camp discipline remained strict. They slept in bell-tents on ground-sheets - no insulated sleeping bags for them. A trench was dug all round the perimeter of each tent to prevent flooding. They loved it to rain in the night, lying listening to it drumming on the canvas adding to the sense of adventure and the illusion that they were 'living rough'.

They would rise with the sun - 4.00am at the height of summer - and go for a swim in the river. It was icy cold, but there was 'no messing - jump in or be chucked in!' Two or three of the best swimmers stood on the banks and in the shallows to make sure no-one got into difficulties, but most of the lads had taught themselves to swim at an early age in Barmston Drain in Swinemoor Lane, known locally as the 'Brickie' and throughout the summer months the scout troop was frequently taken to Atwick on the Holderness coast to swim in the sea.

It was at summer camp that Ernie learned many of his survival skills - what was and what was not edible, how to distinguish between mushrooms, toadstools and other fungi, which berries were palatable and where to find fresh water. They 'played' at manoeuvres, attacking each other's tents at night and capturing each other's flags, learning how to win by stealth and cunning instead of brute force. They helped with the cooking and clearing up and were taught how to look after themselves and keep themselves clean and smart whatever the circumstances.

Abiding memories are of the food ('we ate a helluva lot of Marmite - I've never touched it since'); of sing-songs round the camp-fire when patriotic songs were belted out with more enthusiasm than musical ability; of still larking about at 2.00am even though lights-out was at 10.00pm and reveille at 4.00am and of the comradeship - the friendships forged which were to last a life-time, although in many cases that life-time was to be tragically short. Ernie particularly remembers the Simpson family - Frank, Albert, Les, Joseph and Alf. (They also had a sister, Mary.) Albert was killed in Normandy, and Ernie has since visited his grave. Jack Willison, Billy Holwell, Roland Bielby, Ron Jackson, Billy Scott, Tubby Holmes and Frank Acaster were all good friends, several of whom survivied the war and look back on their scouting days with great affection and gratitiude. Ernie in particular firmly believes that without them he wouldn't be alive to tell this tale.

He stayed with the troop until he left school at the age of fourteen. He had no clear idea of what he wanted to do, even if he'd been allowed the luxury of choosing. He was keen on animals, and would have liked to keep chickens, rabbits, ducks and racing pigeons. He and his friends were for some reason particularly fond of bantams, a fondness he retains to this day. But the overwhelming need was to earn some money and, as the eldest, to supplement the family income. There was no question of taking exams or going on to further education, even if he'd wanted to. In fact the height of his ambition was to 'chase lasses and get a motor-bike.'

His first job was as gardener's boy at a big house called Langholme in New Walk in Beverley. (It's now an Abbeyfield retirement home.) It was owned by the Lambert family and he worked for the widowed Mrs. Frank Lambert who was by then in her eighties. The under gardener, Jim Shingles, lived next door to Ernie's granny and he put in a good word for him. The head gardener was Jack Dean, the chauffeur Arthur Lee, and there were seven servants inside the house. One of them was Betty Ellerington, the kitchen-maid, who was the same age as Ernie and they are still in touch.

The hours were long and the work hard for a fourteen-year-old. His first duties when he arrived at 8.00am had nothing to do with gardening. If there were guests in the house he had to clean their shoes and boots, then fill the seven or eight brass coal-scuttles and take them to their appropriate places, a job he had to repeat before he went home in the evening. (He was also expected to do this at weekends without any extra pay.) After this Betty Ellerington would give Ernie and Jim a cup of coffee which they drank in the shelter of the coal-house in the backyard. Then it was out into the garden where he was mostly employed in digging, or raking the drives and paths. In his lunch hour he was expected to exercise the family's gun dogs after he had eaten his packed lunch. For all this he received the sum of seven shillings and sixpence a week, of which he kept sixpence for himself, giving the rest to his mother. He readily acknowledges that although it helped it didn't anywhere near keep him, as he 'ate like a horse.'

The Lamberts were a good family to work for, despite the seemingly low wages. At Christmas Captain Humphrey Lambert came home from the army and all the staff were entertained to Christmas dinner. Captain Lambert thanked them all and gave them each a bonus of a week's pay. With double wages and a magnificent meal they felt themselves well treated indeed.

After a year at Langholme Ernie's father decided that his son should learn a proper trade and sent him to be an apprentice electrician with a firm called Napier and Wheeldon who were putting electricity into Broadgate Mental Hospital, the local 'lunatic asylum', which was until 1992 situated just outside Beverley Westwood on the Walkington road. Now it's been demolished to make way for new housing. Ernie found it a frightening place, with every door locking automatically behind you, smelling strongly of carbolic soap and disinfectant and with some of the patients kept in straight-jackets or padded cells. Those that were free wore special suits with no buttons, and scared the fifteen-year-old with their strange noises and gestures. The nurses though were kind to him - he remembers Molly Mateer and Nurse Cockin in particular - and some of the patients were allowed out to work in Beverley or on surrounding farms. Some even worked as navvies, but later that practice was stopped. They used to earn enough to contribute to their keep, and the hospital farm also helped towards the costs.

Matron ruled the establishment with a rod of iron and discipline in the hospital was extremely strict. If either matron or the senior nurse approached everybody jumped to attention. Broadgate made a lasting impression on Ernie, even though he was only there for a short time and later when he lived at Walkington he and Doris joined the 'Friends' and worked with and for the staff and patients for many years.

In 1935 Winston Churchill finally persuaded the British Government that they should think seriously about re-arming. One of the resulting projects was the building of a military airfield at Leconfield, three miles north of Beverley on the Driffield road. Ernie's dad heard there was good money to be had there and as well as getting himself a job he found one for Ernie as assistant tea-boy. He worked with a lad called George Barley who eventually became a bookie.

Four to five hundred Irishmen were employed on the site as navvies, constructing the roads and runways. George and Ernie's job was to make tea for them when they knocked off for dinner at noon. George soon decided it was more lucrative to go onto the site and run a book, so Ernie was left in sole charge. His dad told him not to bother with filling the workmen's mugs, but to collect stone jam jars, line them up, fill them with tea and sell them at fourpence a jar. With tips, especially at weekends, he could make about two pounds a week, a great improvement on seven and sixpence and as far as he was concerned a great deal more interesting.

In order to have enough tea ready in time for the workmen he dug a pit across

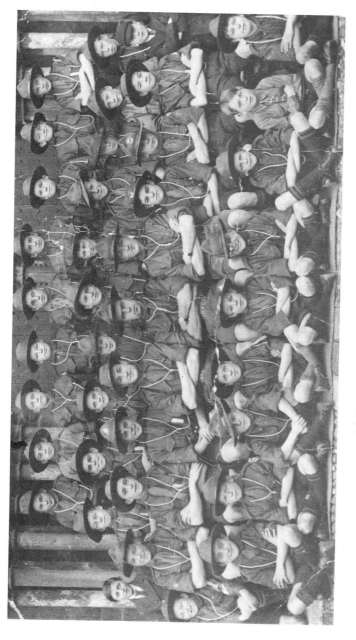

*4th Beverley Minster Scout Troop, 1932.*

*Back row, l. to r.: Roy Tuton, Jack Willinson, Ernie Teal, unknown, Les Banyard, Jack Witty, Ray Lundy, Ray Tyler, Les Christie.*
*2nd row from back, left to right: Roland Bielby, John Thompson, unknown, Bill Simms, John Eldon, F. Constable (?),*
*Frank Acaster, Frank Jones, unknown, Colin Holwell.*
*3rd row from back, left to right: unknown, not in uniform, Albert Simpson, Bill Scott, Ray Thompson, unknown,*
*Rev. S. W. E. Jones, Scoutmaster, Stanley Bell, Assistant Scoutmaster, L. Verity, Stan Warris, Reg Whittaker, Tubby Holmes.*
*Front row, left to right: unknown, Peter Thompson, Les Simpson, Sam Fox, unknown, Chick Verity, Gordon Glenton, unknown,*
*Bob Cherry, S. Fawcett.*

*Old members of 4th Beverley Minster Scout Troop, 1946.*

*Back row, left to right: P. Hugill, R. Jackson, L. Verity, R. Lundie, unknown, unknown, Roland Bielby.*

*Middle row, left to right: Joe Simpson, Ernie Teal, Rev. S. W. E. Jones, Scoutmaster, District Commissioner, Les Christie, John Thompson, Les Simpson.*

*Front row, left to right: unknown, Alf Simpson, R. Lundy (?).*

which he placed iron griddles. Then he collected scrap wood from the joiners who were constructing the hangars, tipped it into the pit and lit it. Six buckets of water were placed on the griddles and when they were boiling a quarter of a pound of tea went into each one along with condensed milk and plenty of sugar. This evil-sounding brew apparently found great favour with the Irishmen.

Despite his relative affluence Ernie decided he could make a bit more money on the side. His constant companion was Laddie, a border collie belonging to a Leconfield farmer called Tommy Wright. In his spare time Ernie used to take Laddie rabbiting and sell the resulting animals for a good profit. One Saturday when he was thus occupied he lost count of the time and to add to his troubles when he did return to his post the wood wouldn't light as it had been raining. The whistle blew for dinner while the water was still only lukewarm and Ernie panicked and ran away. The reason for his precipitate flight was the fate he knew would otherwise overtake him. Misdemeanours on the site were summarily dealt with by throwing the culprit into the communal 'toilet' - a six foot deep pit with a telegraph pole across it! Ernie had no wish to sample the contents of this 'convenience', so jumped on his bike and rode home. Inevitably the foreman, Big Henry, sacked him and once again Ernie was in his father's bad books.

The construction of Leconfield airfield was a great boost for Beverley, providing employment at a time of desperate need. Everything had to be done from scratch - hedges grubbed up, drains and sewers laid and houses, hangars, roads and runways constructed. For Ernie's father it was a Godsend and he wasn't about to let Ernie throw up his chances either. He managed to get him a job with him helping the joiners on the hangars despite in fact that he was in disgrace and had, according to his father, let everybody down. Ernie had no option but to accept although he missed his rabbiting and the extra money.

After working with the joiners for about a month a new man came on site, a six-foot four Irishmen called Macaferty who had a mouth full of gold teeth, and Ernie was assigned to help him. After a couple of weeks Macaferty told him that "Big Henry", the foreman, was going to be sacked and he, Macaferty, would be given the job. Ernie relayed this information to his father, who said not to take any notice - Macaferty was as thick as two short planks. But in fact Big Henry was sacked after an accident in which a workman was killed by a truck in Beverley and Macaferty was given the job of foreman. He appointed Ernie as his assistant to follow him around the site, carrying his briefcase, fetching things for him and making his tea. Ernie describes it as 'a bobby's job.' It lasted two or three months, then his naturally restive nature took over. He took too much for granted, often disappearing to conduct his own activities and frequently when needed was nowhere to be found. Macaferty reluctantly said that although he liked him he thought he'd better go back to working on the hangars.

Ernie's Dad was by this time foreman scaffolder and it was while working with him that Ernie blotted his copy-book finally and irrevocably. Before this however, he was lucky to escape with his life. One day in 1937 they were told that the places would be arriving and they all went up on top of the hangars to watch. The Handley-Page bombers approached and started to circle the airfield. Ernie and his friends were on top of number five hangar and as one plane straightened up ready for landing somebody shouted, "Look out, it's going to hit us." He was told not to be daft as the pilot would know what he was doing. The planes weren't anywhere near as fast as today and it took quite a while to approach, seemingly coming straight for them. Eventually they turned and ran, heading for the back of the roof, as they were seventy feet up and there wasn't time to climb down. The bomber crashed straight into the doors of the hangar, demolishing them completely.

In 1990 Ernie was the guest speaker at a Rotary Club and told the story of the crashing plane as part of his talk. One of the audience said he knew all about it - he had been the rear-gunner! Incidentally one of the scaffolders working with Ernie's dad was Tibby Woodthorpe of Beverley who at the time of writing is still living in the area, aged 94.

Ernie may have escaped with his life after the top-of-the-hangar adventure but it was the same venue that cost him his job. It had been raining and having nothing better to do Ernie, now aged seventeen, was lobbing lumps of concrete over the edge into the puddles seventy feet below. Just as he released one missile somebody stepped out of the hangar doors, took off his cap and scratched his bald head. The lump of concrete scored a direct hit and the unknown man fell to the ground. Ernie strategically withdrew and climbed down the other side of the hangar. As he reached the ground he saw four men carrying the victim away on a shutter-board. Ernie thought he must have killed him and too frightened to say anything, went home for his tea.

Mr. Teal senior was late coming home that evening. Ernie's mum started to fret - he was always on time - where could he be? Just as she was getting really worried a taxi drew up and two men half-carried Ernie's father in. He was white-faced and his head was swathed in bandages. Somebody, he said, had tried to kill him. When he found out who it was, he was going to do the same! Still Ernie kept quiet and turned up for work as usual the next morning, even though he was shaking in his shoes. His dad called together all the men who had been working on that particular hangar the previous day. There were three of them - Tommy Voase, Percy Nolton and Ernie. Closely questioned, Tommy and Percy vehemently denied any involvement. Ernie didn't wait for his turn. Yet again he jumped on his bike but this time, instead of going home, he pedalled straight into Hull, determined to 'join up.'

# Chapter 4

## 'THEY'RE CHANGING THE GUARD . . . . '

Inspired by his time at Leconfield Ernie's first choice of serving his King and country (and evading his father's wrath) was the Royal Air Force. Having talked to the RAF personnel arriving at the new airfield he had decided to be a rear gunner. However he wasn't the only one keen to experience the exhilaration of flying and he was told there was a waiting list of between three and four months. That was no good to Ernie, he needed to get away immediately.

His next port of call was the army recruiting office where there were vacancies, but again there were snags. His choice of regiment was the Coldstream Guards - an ambition harking back to boyhood visits to the Marble Arch cinema. If they came out the back way via Tindall Alley they often encountered Spike Lawson, a huge man dressed in the scarlet tunic of a Coldstream Guardsman and a very romantic figure to the youngsters whose heads were still full of the fantasies recently witnessed on the silver screen. Their arch-enemy 'Chesty', the local policeman, was also an ex-Guardsman and thwarted in his desire to fly Ernie decided that the Guards was the next best thing. However at seventeen he was not a particularly commanding figure. He stood some five foot ten in his socks, just tall enough, but his chest measured only thirty eight inches, one inch under the minimum regulation. Fortunately the Guards were short of recruits and the officer was sympathetic, advising Ernie to take a deep breath and suck in his stomach and they would try again, this time with success. Then followed a medical examination and he was told to go home and wait and they would 'let him know.' The week was spent in wondering what role he could play - could he be a drummer-boy perhaps, or maybe assigned to polishing medals and boots - at least he had experience of that chore. He really didn't care as long as he could wear a scarlet tunic and attract the lasses! His Dad was more practical, pointing out that when he'd served his time he would be eligible for the Police Force or some other secure job, but Ernie wasn't looking that far ahead. His ambitions were more immediate. Within a week he heard that he had been accepted and on November 1st 1937, his eighteenth birthday, he took what was to be a major step in his life. He became a Coldstreamer.

The Guards' London headquarters was in Wellington Barracks near Buckingham Palace but the Guards Depot was at Caterham in Surrey, some miles outside the capital, and it was there that Ernie was told to report on that November day. He had signed on as a 'regular' for four years, plus eight years in the Reserves. He had never travelled further than Bridlington on his own before, so the journey itself was something of an ordeal as well as an adventure, but it was shared by several other recruits who were travelling down on the same day. He particularly remembers a boy from Hull who was joining the Royal Engineers and to whom he talked during the six hours it took to get from Paragon Station to King's Cross.

From London he had to travel by bus to Caterham and the sights and sounds of the city overwhelmed him. The huge buildings, the trams and the cars left him bewildered as he stood with his battered suitcase gazing open-mouthed at the chaotic scene. A man walking by took pity on him and asked him where he wanted to be and on being told 'Caterham' asked if he was joining the Guards. Ernie nodded and received instant sympathy and help. "You poor little b - - - - -. You want such and such a bus, then you change at - Oh come on, I'll take you part of the way." They jumped on a bus, whereupon Ernie was promptly sick. Fortunately as he was still on the platform, he was able to hang out of the back. He put it down to being unused to travelling and being nervous and it was a trait that was to affect him again, albeit in very different circumstances, much later in his life.

His indisposition increased his benefactor's sympathy and he accompanied him all the way to his destination, a one-and-a-half hour journey. When they arrived Ernie shook his hand and thanked him but didn't think to ask his name, so he has remained unknown.

Clutching his pass Ernie walked through the entrance gates to the depot and was immediately challenged by the sentry, who took him to the guard-room where he was asked his name by the fearsome-looking soldier on duty. "Ernie Teal," he said nervously, which obviously enraged his inquisitor. "What do you think these are - Mars bars?" he roared, pointing to his sleeve. "When you speak to me say 'Sergeant!'" Shades of things to come!

He was taken to the reception centre by his escort who set off 'at a helluva pace - like the clappers'. On enquiring what the hurry was he was told to shut up - talking wasn't allowed. You only spoke when you were spoken to. In the reception centre he was greeted by a 'Trained Soldier'. He knew this because not only did it say so on his sleeve badge but he was told that when he addressed him it was to be 'Yes Trained Soldier' and 'No Trained Soldier'. Ernie's already battered spirits sank even lower.

He was told to remove his civvies and get into the bath, scrub himself down and get dressed in the denims which were unceremoniously thrown to him. He was asked for his address, and his civilian clothes were parcelled up and posted home. Ernie Teal, aged exactly eighteen, was transformed at that moment into Guardsman Teal, a title he was to keep for the next nine years.

Washed and dressed, Ernie was given supper and shown to his sleeping quarters where he tumbled into bed and fell immediately into an exhausted sleep. What seemed to him to be a short time later he was woken by bugles. Assuming it was the middle of the night he at first thought there must be a fire, but just as he was wondering what he should do about it he was tipped unceremoniously out of bed by not one but several Trained Soldiers. He wasn't singled out for this treatment, it was administered quite impartially to everyone in the hut. "That's Reveille," they were told. "As soon as you hear that - out!"

More recruits joined them during the next two or three days and when the complement reached thirty they were marched down to 13 Company Coldstream Guards. They assembled in a barrack room where they were introduced to the Drill and Squad Sergeants, two Corporals and two Trained Soldiers. The Sergeant's words were presumably meant to inspire them. He would, he said, kill half of them, but the half that remained would be good soldiers. They were told how to address the Officers and NCO's then marched away to be kitted out and have their regulation short back and sides. Next it was to the dentist where Ernie had seven teeth filled, which he still has nearly sixty years later. Not that he enjoyed the experience. He had vivid memories of the somewhat rough and ready methods of the school dentist and when in later years he again needed some attention to his teeth he was much relieved to find that he could have 'gas'. Unfortunately he reacted badly to it and came round to find that he had wrestled the poor dentist to the floor!

The next few weeks were a non-stop round of activities punctuated by brief intervals of sleep - reveille, P.T. in the gymnasium, climbing ropes, jumping horses, drill, drill and more drill. The Trained Soldier taught them to look after their equipment. He would suddenly appear in an evening and shout 'Boots clean'. When you thought they were you had to take them to him and if he didn't agree he would throw them out through the window into the barrack square and you had to retrieve them one at a time in your mouth like a Labrador dog. It was all in the call of discipline, to teach instant obedience without question. There were, inevitably, objections. One such objector (a big man with size fourteen boots according to Ernie) had the temerity to answer back. He was promptly dragged out, stripped, and scrubbed with yard-brushes under a cold shower. 'You can't buck the army,' they were told. 'No matter how big you are we will subdue you!' Now of course it's different. In the modern technological warfare the accent is on brains rather than brawn, but instant discipline is still an essential part of a soldier's training. As Coldstream Guards all the drill they were taught was in direct preparation for duty outside Buckingham Palace and for Trooping the Colour on the Sovereign's official birthday. Ernie was to take part in this ceremony twice. In 1938 the Duke of Gloucester took the parade, but in 1939 it was King George VI. He still thinks no other country in the world can put on a better spectacle and never misses watching it on television.

After six months at Caterham, during which many fell by the wayside, the recruits were considered fit to be shown to the world. They travelled by train to Waterloo Station where they were met by army trucks. Ernie marvelled again at the traffic and the buildings as they drove down the Mall, past Buckingham Palace to Wellington Barracks, where they lined up in the square. A huge Regimental Sergeant Major was there to greet them - RSM Brittain - the biggest man with the loudest voice in the whole of the British army. Eventually of course he became famous, but in those days his talents were confined to the Coldstream Guards. He walked along the lines inspecting this new batch of raw material. When he came to Ernie he put out his arm at shoulder level, over the top of Ernie's head. "They're sending us little ones now are they?" he bellowed, "How old are you? Eighteen? You'll grow - we'll make the best of you."

Ernie was impressed. RSM Brittain, he says, gleamed. At twenty-four stones he weighed more than twice Ernie's ten stone three and his physical presence dominated the scene. He had medals from the first world war and never demanded more of his men than he was prepared to give.

The Guards were divided into four companies, numbers one and four were big men, numbers two and three (Ernie's) the relatively small. His Company Commander was Lord Frederick Cambridge, cousin to the King, and the Commanding Officer was Colonel Bingham, father of the notorious Lord Lucan.

Ernie's first taste of public duty was with the St. James' Palace Guard outside Marlborough House, the home of Queen Mary the Queen Mother. She was very strict and insisted on everything being just so. He was put on double sentry duty with an 'old soldier' just back from Palestine and with ten years service behind him. Ernie started off putting into practice all the things he'd been taught - march towards each other, salute in unison, present arms, count your steps, stamp your feet. They did two hours on and four hours off and during their first break his fellow guardsman advised him not to work so hard. "Civilians don't know the difference between correct procedures and taking it easy," he said. "You won't last the guard out if you go on stamping your feet and swinging your arms like that - you'll kill yourself." Taking his advice, Ernie left out all the crisp movements he'd been taught and was just congratulating himself on learning the ropes when he saw his companion snap to attention and start stamping and swinging with gusto. Unbeknown to him RSM Brittain had decided to combine an evening stroll with his wife with a look at his 'new boys'!

When Ernie returned to the barracks at the end of his period on duty he was 'fell in' with an escort, his rifle and bayonet were confiscated and he was 'put where the birds couldn't sh - - on him' - a favourite barrackroom expression. Next day he was taken from his cell and marched in front of the Company Commander. RSM Brittain wanted to make an example of him. "He's only just joined and already he's slopping about," he complained. "Talk about idle on sentry duty - never seen anything like it in all my life." But Colonel Bingham (the only Socialist Peer in the Brigade of Guards) was more understanding, saying he thought Ernie had been led astray. He got off relatively lightly with five days CB.

All things are relative and those five days were in reality hell on earth. There were always a fair number of culprits on CB at any one time and as soon as reveille sounded they had to be out on the square on their hands and knees picking up every matchstick and tab end and not until every last tiny scrap had been removed could they get up off their hands and knees and march to the cookhouse to scrub out all the pans. After that it was at the double back to their barrack room to wash and shave before breakfast.

When the bugler sounded the call 'You can be a defaulter as long as you like  as long as you answer your name,' they had to run out onto the square no matter what time of day or night it was or what they were doing. They had always been taught to listen for the bugle, which regulated their lives. Now it dominated them. At 3.00pm they paraded on the square for an hour's drill instruction wearing puttees and with a full pack, blanket and full waterbottle. One day RSM Brittain came out with a gleam in his eye and instructed the two Sergeants and the Corporal to march the men round the back so that they couldn't be seen by members of the public through the railings. "I don't want any b - - - - - writing to the Daily Mirror", he said. The Sergeant was told to 'teach these men a lesson they'll never forget. If there's a single one still standing up in half an hour I'll bust you as well.' But Ernie, as he'd said before, was tough. The men had to quick march with rifles above their heads non-stop, turning, counter-marching and double time. The sweat poured off them and most gave up. But Ernie was very fit - he didn't drink or smoke and what's more he was determined not to give in, even though they kept tightening his belt to wind him. Eventually the Sergeant who was 'a decent bloke' said, "Look lad - I don't want to kill you, and I don't want to get busted. If you won't go down I'll have to knock you down."

By the time RSM Brittain returned they were all flat out. He called them to attention and told them it was for their own good. "When you are on Palace Guard

*After one month in the army,
at the Guards Depot,
Caterham, in 1937.
(Ernie is on the left.)*

*Early 1939 before the
outbreak of war.*

*On a recruitment drive outside the Cecil Cinema in 1938. (2nd right, back row.)*

or anywhere else on public duty you represent not only your regiment but your country. There are a lot of German tourists in London. If they see you slopping about as Guardsmen they'll think we're a bigger push-over than we are. You are there to do a job. You'll do it or die in the attempt." The year was 1938.

Despite the unsettled state of world politics it was a very exciting time for an eighteen-year-old to be in London. He stood guard at Buckingham Palace, St. James' Palace, the Bank of England, the Tower of London and Windsor Castle. He took part in many State Visits, including being a member of the Guard of Honour for President Le Blum of France and his wife when they were presented at Court. King George VI was ill so his Consort Queen Elizabeth (now the Queen Mother) officiated. As they waited for her to come into the Inner Quadrangle the full battalion of a thousand men were 'standing easy'. Someone was supposed to press a button to warn the Captain of the Guard that the Queen was on her way but it didn't work. The first he knew was when he turned round and saw the Queen walking between the ranks who were still standing easy. He quickly called them to attention but it was too late. There was, says Ernie, one helluva row!

One night a mentally disturbed man climbed into the gardens of the Palace despite the barbed wire topping the walls which surrounded the forty acres. Ernie and his fellow guardsmen were taking their ease in the guardroom between spells of duty and, strictly against regulations, had removed their boots. When the Sergeant rushed in and commanded, "Turn out - prowler in the grounds," there was a mad rush to put them on and grab their rifles. There were by this time policemen on every wall-top and the man was quickly arrested.

The variety and responsibility of the duties Ernie was assigned to matured him from the raw 'country bumpkin' into a disciplined soldier. He had of course attained his ambition of a scarlet tunic, plus a bearskin, and he found it had the desired effect on 'the lasses'. They would stand and admire the precision of the movements of the two guardsmen outside the palace gates who seemingly without any commands did everything in unison. In reality it was all down to the rifle butt and was decided by the right hand man. One tap for 'patrol', two for 'salute', three for 'present arms'. One tap on the butt meant come to attention, one pace forward with sloped arms, turn to face each other, march towards each other then march out and back again, all in step. Easy when you know how!

As well as guarding the Royal Palaces the Coldstreamers took turns at mounting the guard on the Bank of England. Twenty-four Guardsmen with two Corporals, one Sergeant and an Officer would march to the Bank from either Chelsea or Wellington Barracks - a considerable distance. One officer with plenty of money used to march his squad to St. James' Tube Station, give them the order to 'un-fix bayonets' then march them onto the train where they sat in full uniform to the astonishment of the other passengers. They would disembark at 'Bank' fix bayonets and complete the journey on foot.

The Officer was always invited to dine at the Bank and could invite a guest to join him at the six-course dinner. Most of them seemed to choose 'a titled young lady!' Unlike the Royal Guard which was two hours on and four hours off Bank Guard was one on and two off, as they must always be on the alert. The main guard was on the bullion room. There were no double sentries, each Guardsman was in a separate room. Despite the responsbility and the difficulties of getting there it was a popular duty as each man was issued with a brand new shilling, fresh from the Mint, on arrival and the bank had its own little canteen where crisps, lemonade or a cup of tea could be bought. The other unusual duty was at the Magazine in Hyde Park which held all the ammunition for the London Garrisons, including the Artillery. It was guarded by twenty-four men day and night.

The Coldstreams of course were an infantry battalion but the Life Guards and the Royal Horse Guards were mounted. As they passed the foot guards they would blow their bugles in salute and in return the foot guards would be called to attention and present arms. When on Royal sentry duty the Guardsmen were always visited during the hours of darkness by a patrol led by a drummer-boy carrying a hurricane lamp. The patrol consisted of four Guardsmen, one Corporal, one Sergeant and an Officer. They would halt at each sentry post and the officer would ask what their orders were and to whom did they present arms? The correct reply was, 'The Sovereign, all members of British and foreign Royal Families, Heads of State, King's Guard, King's Lifeguard and all armed Corps.' Ernie can still rattle it off today. The King's Guard was the incoming foot-guard, the King's Lifeguard were mounted.

Night duty gave the Officers a chance to talk to the young Guardsmen whom they rarely saw during the day, and also to have a bit of fun at their expense by asking awkward questions. Ernie's Company Commander was Lord Frederick Cambridge, who was always on Palace Guard, and he knew he must always be ready for unusual questions from him. One night after the ritual 'Name' (Guardsman Teal No. 2658082 Sir) ' What are your orders?' (Present arms to . . . . etc.) he asked, "If an enemy battleship came steaming down the Mall with all its guns firing what would you do Teal?" "Sir," he replied, "sink down into my boots and fire through the lace-holes," a reply which both satisfied and amused the King's cousin.

Each day at 5.00am the Royal dustman would come through the gates to empty the Royal dustbins. He was a little fellow with a bowler hat - Ernie thought he looked like an Irishman. He smoked a pipe and the Guardsmen always presented arms to him. They would also honour their own or any especially pretty young ladies in the same way. The Police would tip them off when Royalty were approaching so that they would be ready to present arms to them.

There were of course, in spite of the strict discipline, lapses of conduct among these lively young men. One hot night the sentries took off their boots and paddled in the Victoria Fountain. The King took particular exception to this prank and the culprits were put under close arrest, although the young Officer thought it was 'jolly good fun.' Another time during a debutantes' ball two Guardsmen were caught on a balcony watching a Lady-in-Waiting preparing for bed. Not only were they punished but the Captain got into trouble for allowing it to happen.

The highlight of the Guardsmen's year was of course the annual ceremony of Trooping the Colour in honour of the Sovereign's 'official' birthday in June. The official birthday was created in order to be able - as far as possible - to avoid inclement weather conditions. Every battalion in London took part - five or six of them each with 1,240 men. Only cooks and batmen were excused. For weeks before the actual day they would set off each morning at 5.00am to march to Horseguards Parade for rehearsals.

In June 1939 the 1st Battalion Coldstream Guards were to receive new Colours. RSM Brittain was to accept them from King George VI who was a very slight man.

His Majesty was heard to remark to one of his aides that he was afraid the six foot four Guardsman was going to jump on top of him as he took a great pace forward and snatched the colours! In those days if a Guardsman fainted on parade at the Colour ceremony he was left lying there and his comrades had to step over him. Later he would be put on CB, however hot the day and whatever excuse he offered. Trying to ease aching limbs and restricted blood-vessels by transferring the weight to the balls of the feet earned an instant reprimand for fidgeting. Nowadays more humane rules are applied and any unfortunate victims are stretchered unobtrusively away. Ernie, being small, was always at the left of the ranks on parade, the tallest men being on the right. It was the man on the right who determined the timing for fixing bayonets. On the command 'Fix' he would take seven sharp paces forward and come to attention. On the command 'Bayonets' he pushed the bayonet straight out, looked to see everybody had stopped 'fiddling about' then thrust it up into the air and onto the rifle. Back at the barracks it was the turn of the smallest man to reverse the procedure.

In between the public spectacles everyday life was often harsh and was run by strict codes of conduct which must not be transgressed. Each layer in the hierarchy - NCO's, Sergeants, Corporals, etc. - had their own mess and there was no fraternisation. There was a great deal of bullying and punishments were terrible and often pointless. Huge barrack-room floors had to be scrubbed white then polished again by hand by anyone on CB to teach them to do as they were told. The discipline has stayed with Ernie throughout his life. He hates litter, notices hair-cuts and cannot abide unpunctuality. He thinks it was a good regime on the whole that paid off in the long run and that if more sections of the armed forces had followed the example set by the Guards, the Marines, and the first class county regiments such as the East Yorkshires and the Green Howards it would have helped them in the subsequent fighting against the highly disciplined German troops.

If life in the Guards was tough, Ernie was even tougher. He loved it and relished each new experience. Joining up was, he says, the best thing he ever did in his life - apart from marrying Doris of course.

# Chapter 5

## WITH THIS RING . . . .

On September 23rd 1941 Nellie Doris Martha Williams promised to love, honour and obey George Ernest Teal as long as they both should live. Fifty years on she could be said to have fulfilled her part of the contract in full measure as the couple celebrated their Golden Wedding surrounded by their families and with cards and presents from literally hundreds of well-wishers.

Like any other marriage it has had its ups and downs during the fifty years, not least because husband and wife came from very different backgrounds. Ernie is descended from generations of country folk, while Doris is a Londoner. She was born in 1920 in Kennington about three-quarters of a mile from three of the Royal Parks - St. James', Green and Hyde. One of five children she had two brothers - one four years older than herself, the other two years younger - and two sisters. Gladys was four years her junior but Margaret was very much an afterthought, being born some eleven years after Doris. Mr. Williams drove a London bus, and the family were reasonably well off, living in a big Victorian house with a garden in Walcot Square about half a mile from the Oval cricket ground. Doris's maternal grandparents lived in Camden Town near Regent's Park, just a bus-ride away from Kennington, but she never knew her father's family, from whom he had inherited the Walcot Square house. The Williams children were very strictly brought up. They attended a church school during the week and were sent to Sunday school twice on each Sabbath, dressed in their Sunday best. The only recreation allowed on Sundays was a family walk in the evening through one of the Royal Parks, an activity Doris remembers with pleasure. Bands would be playing and there was 'a very nice atmosphere' of warmth and friendliness.

Walcot Square was a pleasant place to live, with its central garden full of trees and with space for the children to play sedate games. In those days most of the residents were working class. Now the area has become fashionable and many of the substantial double fronted houses are occupied by MP's and businessmen. There was a view of Big Ben and they used to look to see if the light was on, which meant Parliament was sitting. Mr. Williams' word was law. On Sundays he would carve the joint at a set time, and woe betide anyone who wasn't punctual.

Doris started school when she was three and stayed at the same one until she was fourteen. She felt she was lucky to be the eldest girl as the middle sister, Gladys, used to have to wear her cast-off clothes and also look after the 'baby', Margaret. By the age of ten Doris avers that she had learnt the basics and that the four years after that were wasted. She would have liked to have gone on to College to learn craft work but it was too expensive. There were no grants - all higher education had to be paid for - and with five children to educate a bus driver's wage just wasn't enough for luxuries like college. However, Doris's talents didn't go to waste. Her maternal grandmother had a dressmaking business in the West End so her mother - although no needlewoman herself - decided that young Doris would follow in Grandma's footsteps. She was already skilled in embroidery and so at fourteen she was apprenticed to a Court Dressmaker called Madame Sarlette in Hanover Square, just off Regent Street. It wasn't easy to get an apprenticeship in the 1930's but armed with an excellent recommendation from her school Doris, shaking with terror, set off on the tube for her interview with the formidable Madame. She was offered a five-year apprenticeship, which she accepted with some trepidation, and was set to work in the lowliest job of all, retrieving pins with a magnet after the cleaners had swept the workroom floors. Another task for the younger members of the staff was to ask each seamstress what materials she needed from the stock-room, write the list of items down carefully on a note-pad then go and get them.

Madame Sarlette made gowns for many members of the aristocracy and occasionally when they came in for a fitting she would phone upstairs for the appropriate garment to be taken down to the salon. The apprentices would vie with each other for this honour so that they could catch a glimpse of the grey-carpeted splendour with its glittering chandeliers and gilt furniture which Doris thought was the last word in elegance. They had to take great care that they weren't seen, otherwise they wouldn't be allowed downstairs again.

Doris enjoyed her work, learning new skills and techniques as she was assigned to the various departments, each specialising in different components - sleeves, bodices, skirts, etcetera. By the end of the apprenticeship not only did they have to known how to construct each one from scratch but how to put them all together into a finished garment. At first she was paid seven shillings and sixpence a week. By 1939 this had increased to the magnificent sum of twelve shillings and sixpence. She just managed to complete her apprenticeship before the war put an end to the ball-gown trade and the workrooms were turned over to the production of uniforms, but by then she had her precious Certificate of Proficiency - similar to today's City and Guilds qualification.

During her time at Madame Sarlette's Doris's talent for embroidery was put to full use. Dresses for debutantes for their Court presentations were much in demand. Regulations for these gowns were very strict. Backs must be no lower than a certain specified measurement and trains and feathers had to be just so, but the hand-embroidery could be as flamboyant as you could afford, with bead work being in great demand. For the basic construction sewing machines were used, but Doris had been there for three years before a mechanical overlocker was purchased. Before that every seam had to be oversewn by hand to prevent fraying. Patterns were also traced by hand onto the beautiful materials and a dress could cost as much as a hundred and fifty pounds, a fortune compared to the wages of those who had created it. Doris would sometimes take home waste scraps of material to show to her mother and sisters.

The young seamstresses all got on well together and used to meet socially as well as at work. During the lunch-break they would window-shop in Oxford Street and Regent Street and every week they each put a little of their meagre wages into a kitty so that at six-weekly intervals they could visit the nearby Palladium to see a show. At weekends they would meet for walks in the park and it was during one such walk with her cousin that Doris met her fate in the shape of a young Coldstream Guardsman called George Ernest Teal. She was seventeen, three years into her apprenticeship, and he was just a year older.

From the first there was a language difficulty. London born and bred, Doris couldn't understand a word of Ernie's broad Yorkshire dialect. She thought he said he came from Goole. But there must have been something about him that attracted her. He was in uniform when they first met but subsequently turned up to meet her in a variety of suits which impressed her enormously. She decided he must have 'a bit of money' to be always so smartly dressed. She was soon to be disillusioned.

The initial uniform issued to the Guardsmen was free - scarlet tunic, blue tweed trousers with a red stripe down each side-seam, blue-grey cape and a peaked forage cap with a brass trim. An NCO had three brass strips on his cap brim. They were also 'loaned' bearskins for the duration of their service but they remained public property. In those days they really were bearskins, made from the pelts of the Canadian grizzly. Nowadays they are synthetic fur. Unlike the rest of the uniform they weren't made to measure. You just had to go through the available stock and select the best fit possible and hopefully one with a good 'tail'. They were inferior to those of the officers which were much taller and with lovely sleek 'tails'. Once issued, the bearskin remained the responsibility of the individual guardsman until he left the service and was kept on his locker-top on a special stand. It had to be kept well-groomed, with the curb-chain polished with Bluebell polish which cost a shilling a tin. Bearskins were worn when mounting guard and on ceremonial occasions, including rehearsals for Trooping the Colour. Hot and heavy they contributed to the physical demands of the duties and to the occasional collapse of men not in the peak of condition.

After the first issue all subsequent uniforms had to be paid for. A scarlet tunic cost six guineas, a considerable sum when the clothing allowance was three shillings and sixpence a week. Having attained his boyhood ambition of wearing one Ernie was keen to show it off to Doris when he first started courting her. On one occasion when they were walking in Hyde Park it began to rain. Ever the gentleman Ernie put his cape round Doris, which meant that his scarlet tunic got wet through. Unlike modern materials it stained and the next time he reported for guard duty the Adjutant and RSM, who inspected them before each turn out, ordered 'tunic stopped.' It was not to be worn again and he must order another one which he must pay for himself. As a young recruit he had only saved a small amount in the 'bank', so the rest was lent to him and had to be paid back out of his wages at the rate of eight shillings a week. As his total pay was only ten shillings it left him very short of cash. Out of his remaining two shillings he had to buy his Bluebell button polish, razor blades, soap and toothpaste, which left practically nothing with which to impress Doris!

One way he economised was to swap his soap. When it was getting to the end of its useful life he would go into the wash-house, select his victim from among the thirty or forty guardsmen attending to their ablutions, wait until he was 'well lathered-up' and couldn't see, then swap his sliver of soap for the unfortunate man's new tablet. Ernie would then move smartly down the line and with luck somebody else would get the blame.

Sometimes he was on the receiving end of similar ploys such as the day when somebody pinched his Bluebell. Ernie was by far the smallest and lightest in his room and as such considered by some to be fair game, but as we have said before, he was tough. He demanded to known who the culprit was, threatening to wrap his Bondook rifle round the neck of the guilty party. Crab Wilson, a big tough old soldier with a broken nose who after the war starred as a paratrooper in the film 'The Longest

*Doris's father, Bill Williams, standing by "his" bus, probably about 1918*
*when he was a conductor.*

*The Williams Family.*
*Back row, left to right: Doris, Reg and Gladys.*
*Front row, left to right: Nell, Bill and Margaret.*

*Nell and Bill Williams in later life.*

*Beverley Minster, September 23rd, 1941.*
*Left to right: Muriel Teal, best man Eddie Ewen, Ernie, Doris,*
*Bill Williams, Gladys Williams.*

*Ernie and Doris outside Beverley Minster, September 23rd, 1941.*

Day', threw his rifle at Ernie and said, "I took your polish. There's your rifle, here's my chin - what are you going to do about it?" Ernie showed him, whereupon he got up off the floor and hit Ernie back, but after that despite his small stature he was treated with a great deal more respect.

There were ways of acquiring more funds of course. The money-lenders were only too willing to help you out of a temporary difficulty by lending you five shillings to take your young lady out. They would be waiting when the recruits collected their pay, ready to pounce on anyone who had had it docked for some reason. The trouble was they charged threepence a week on every shilling, so after one week the five shillings had become six and threepence, which was impossible to pay back out of two shillings, and so it went on mounting up. Once they got a grip on you it was difficult to break free.

When you had been in the Guards for twelve months you could apply to wear civilian clothes when off duty. You had to march in in your pin-stripe suit and bowler hat to be inspected. Still without funds Ernie in desperation borrowed a suit from a friend and duly had his pass stamped with the magic words "allowed to wear civilian clothes." It was this borrowed finery which so impressed Doris, as he went the rounds of his friends each time he went out. There were occasions of course when all suitable suits were being worn and Ernie had to meet Doris in uniform. This didn't please her as she said her father wouldn't approve of her walking out with a Guardsman. Next evening he walked to Walcot Square and knocked on the door of Doris's house. Her father opened it and was greeted by Ernie with, "Excuse me - are you Mr. Williams?" On agreeing that he was Ernie went on, "I understand you don't like your daughter being courted by a Guardsman." The reply was unexpected. "Which daughter? I've got three." On being told it was Doris he protested that he had no idea what he was talking about and invited him in. After that Ernie was welcomed into the family home whenever he wished, regularly going there for his Sunday dinner when he wasn't on duty.

One day he went straight there after being on guard all morning. His boots were white with sweat after several hours of marching and stamping and in the warmth of the dining room they soon began to smell. As Doris's father was carving the joint he suddenly demanded that the family cat to be put outside as it smelled terrible. Ernie wished it would come back in as of course the awful aroma remained and eventually he had to confess that he was the culprit!

Still with no money, Ernie's courting consisted mostly of walks in the park, but he did eventually, after saving hard for three weeks, manage to get together enough to take Doris to the cinema. They went to the Grand in the Edgeware Road, where the price of a seat even in those days was three shillings. With Ernie resplendent in full uniform complete with swagger cane they queued to go in, saw the film and were coming out down the staircase when Ernie slipped and in full view of the queue for the second house went head-first from top to bottom. Pride certainly went before that fall. By Christmas of his first year of courtship Ernie's weekly wages had crept back up to three shillings and sixpence, so he was able to buy Doris a gift of perfume. Unfortunately he chose the glamorously dark-blue and silver packaged "Evening in Paris" which she thought smelled awful!

Despite all these set-backs the relationship betweenErnie and Doris strengthened and deepened and when she was nineteen and he was twenty they were formally engaged. He was by this time fighting in France, but was given home leave in January 1940 and decided to collect Doris from London and take her to Beverley to meet his parents. They travelled to Hull on a train packed with soldiers also going home on leave, arriving at midnight after an eight hour journey to find snow and fog adding to the hazards of the blackout. They had missed the last train to Beverley and there were no taxis running so they decided to spend the night in the waiting room. However, the rowdy behavious of the soldiers sharing their temporary shelter upset Ernie, intent on making a good impression on his young lady, so they set off to walk the eight miles home. Doris had no idea how far it was and soon found that her best clothes and high-heeled shoes which she was wearing in honour of this first meeting with her future in-laws were entirely unsuitable for the snow-bound roads of East Yorkshire.

They walked for ages, the fog so dense visibility was down to a mere yard or two. They met a man who asked them where they were going and when they told him he was so sorry for them he gave them his torch. They stumbled on, Doris with her suitcase, Ernie with kit-bag, rifle and tin helmet. They were, to quote Doris, 'in a right pickle.' Eventually they stopped while Doris changed her shoes for a sturdier pair from her case and Ernie opened the bottle of wine he had brought back from France for his parents and they had a drink to warm them up and keep them going.

They had got as far as Woodmansey, some three miles outside Beverley, when they heard a car approaching from behind. Ernie flagged it down to find it was full of servicemen some of whom he recognised. He asked whether they could give his young lady a lift, and somehow they fitted her in on somebody's knee - to this day she has no idea who he was. Relieved of his luggage as well, Ernie trudged along by the side of the car as it crawled through the fog into Beverley town. Visibility was so bad that they went right past his home without recognising it, but eventually they stumbled in at a quarter past four in the morning, Doris with her hair covered in icicles and her best clothes ruined.

Her first impressions of Ernie's beloved Yorkshire were not improved by finding herself in a tiny dark and old-fashioned cottage whose inhabitants were all asleep in bed! Ernie's mother had prepared a lovely meal and waited up for hours but had eventually decided they weren't coming. However, when they did meet they got on very well, although Doris still found the gas-lights with their hanging chains, the oak beams and the little brown sink in the corner of the living room very different from home - 'a real old spot' she recalls. By the time she and Ernie moved in after the war it had been refurbished and had electricity installed, but at that time of course they had no idea that it was to be their future home.

Ernie and Doris were married in Beverley Minster on September 23rd 1941, when Doris was twenty one. She had by then been living in Beverley with Ernie's parents on and off for about two years. When Madame Sarlette's changed from making court dresses to making uniforms she could have stayed on and been exempt from being drafted into war work. She really wanted to join the forces, but Ernie was having none of either of these things. He wanted her out of London, safe in Yorkshire away from the blitz. Had he known the fate Hull was to suffer he might not have been so insistent. However, she dutifully took up residence at 6, Highgate, and got a job in Armstrong's factory, just round the corner in Eastgate, making shells.

She found it a strange life at first, although she says that Ernie's mother was very good to her. But as well as the tiny old-fashioned house and the quietness of the small market town she missed her family and friends and the fun she had had and longed to go back home. She soon made new friends, and they did have fun, but the Beverley girls were very different from the ones she'd left behind. When the bombing of Hull started they frequently had to leave the factory and crowd into the shelters, but at least they still had a roof over their heads. When she went back to Walcot Square on a visit she found the roof off and the windows blasted in.

Doris borrowed her sister-in-law's dress for her September wedding, so as war-time nuptials went it was a relatively splendid affair with the bride in white and the groom in battledress. Family and friends donated clothing coupons so that Doris could buy enough material to make bridesmaids' dresses for her sister Gladys and Ernie's sister Muriel and London's thriving black market provided the ingredients for the wedding cake. As long as you had the money you could buy almost anything. To Doris's abiding sorrow her parents decided that they couldn't risk the journey to Hull for the ceremony, but her elder brother, on leave from the army, came to give her away and her sister travelled up on the train carrying the precious cake. As usual it was very crowded and she spent the entire journey worrying about it getting damaged.

Apart from the black market, food was of course strictly rationed, but Ernie's mother had made spam sandwiches and with the cake and some wine they managed a small reception. Flowers were ordered from the Ladygate Nurseries of J. Sellars and Son and cost one pound fourteen shillings and sixpence. The day was recorded for posterity by the photographer T. Hollingsworth of North Bar Within. His bill was for two pounds and nine shillings.

Although Doris says it was a 'nice little wedding' the regret that her parents weren't there to share it lingers to this day.

# Chapter 6

## INTO BATTLE

When Ernie joined the army he didn't give a great deal of thought to the implications. He was attracted by the scarlet tunic and by the idea of maybe playing a drum or blowing a bugle, but certainly didn't equate the Guards with fighting. It was also by chance that Hull and Beverley were recruiting areas for the Coldstreams - a northern regiment - and at that time he knew nothing about their history. Gradually he was to learn about their battle honours and to become extremely proud to be a member of such an illustrious band.

As young Guardsmen they were regularly questioned about the battle honours displayed on the walls above their beds in Wellington Barracks. If an officer walked in and said, "State Battle Honours," they were expected to be able to go through the details of each encounter which had resulted in the awards so displayed. For example if they were asked, "Who was the bravest man in the British Army?" they had to be able to tell the story of a Lance-Corporal who defended his position in a French farm. The British had retreated into the farmyard, closing the two big gates behind them, but the locking bar was missing. The Lance-Corporal put his arm through the slots and held on despite a battering ram being used by the enemy. Eventually they had to cut his arm in half to get in and he was posthumously awarded the Victoria Cross for his bravery and endurance. Wellington used to say, 'You'll always find the Guards where the fighting is hardest'.

During the Civil War the Coldstreams declared themselves for Cromwell and although they subsequently marched down to London and laid down their arms, swearing allegiance to King Charles, they are still the only regiment not allowed to include a crown on their buttons or cap badges. King Charles eventually praised them as 'second only to the Grenadiers.' Ernie of course doesn't agree! As far as he is concerned their motto is the truth - 'Second to None.'

As in some schools, sporting ability was held in higher regard in the Guards than academic ability. If you could play football (either soccer or rugby) or cricket or run or box your popularity both with the officers and with your fellow soldiers was assured. Ernie was more than happy to play soccer, but not so thrilled about he annual Guards' boxing tournament. Everyone was expected to take part. There were no different weight categories, opponents were just drawn out of a hat. It took place in a huge gymnasium and RSM Brittain was very much in evidence using his great voice to encourage the representatives of his regiment.

Ernie was drawn against a Guardsman called Sewell of the King's Company Grenadiers. The qualification for that regiment included a minimum height of six foot two. Ernie, weighing in at ten stone three, decided to go and seek him out before the tournament and throw himself on his mercy, so went to his barracks and asked for him. He was pointed in the general direction of the barrack room and on entering the first person he saw was, 'a big hairy b - - - - - sitting on a bed.' This did indeed prove to be his opponent, but when Ernie told him he'd been drawn against him in the novice boxing he received scant sympathy. "Tough luck you poor b - - - - -. I'll have to make a fight of it." And make a fight of it he did. Ernie of course applied the same principle as he had when he was on CB - a flat refusal to lie down. He was several stones lighter than his opponent and afterwards all he remembered was walking towards him and the next instant being flat on his back looking up at the ceiling with a pain in his neck. He got up, not realising he'd been hit and was promptly knocked down again. This procedure was repeated several times until he was carried back to his corner. Next day on parade he was dismissed and confined to his quarters until the swelling on his face had subsided and the black and blue bruising had faded to a respectable yellow.

There were of course inklings of the more serious fighting to come when once a year the regiment went on manoeuvres to Purbright or Salisbury Plain for a month. They were issued with a new experimental kind of battledress which they had to test out. It was eventually modified to become the standard issue for active service. Ernie enjoyed these spells away from London, remembering not only the actual exercises with the officers 'galloping about like Red Indians,' but also for the first time hearing the song of the nightingale. Occasionally during 1939 the young Guardsmen were gathered together for a talk by an officer about a man called Adolf Hitler, but it meant very little to these eighteen and nineteen-year-olds intent on enjoying life to the full. As far as they were concerned Hitler looked like Charlie Chaplin. In August 1939 the Battalion left London for their training ground in Purbright in Surrey. On September 3rd. Britain declared war on Germany.

The men were gathered together in a cinema on that late summer Sunday and an official from the Foreign Office tried to explain to them why the declaration of war had finally been made. He said it was important that the regular soldiers should know what they were going to fight - and possibly die - for. Most of the men gathered there on that afternoon would subsequently die, but at that time not many of them understood what it was all about. After the official had been talking for nearly an hour he asked if there were any questions. One joker stood up and said, "Yes sir - can you tell me why we're going to war?" He was immediately put under close arrest, but it summed up the general feeling of unreality prevailing at the time.

The regiment was put onto a war footing and a week later they were again gathered in the cinema to meet their Divisional Commander, a Major General by the name of Montgomery, who was in command of the Third Infantry Division. He gave them 'a real talking to' and made them all 'perk up' - a very different approach from the previous week. He marched onto the stage and barked, "Cough!" Then, "Stop! No more coughing and no smoking. Next week I am going to take you into France." Montgomery was at that time almost unknown and looked down on by the Guards Officers who called him the "The Little Man."

On September 22nd. the Third Infantry Division embarked from Southampton, landing at Cherbourg. Their month's manoeuvres, even though they had used live ammunition, had done little to prepare them for the actual fighting. They were still mostly very young, hardly more than boys and had been trained almost exclusively as ceremonial troops. For most of them it was their first time abroad. There were a few old soldiers who had served in Palestine and Egypt and knew their way about - especially among the brothels and the 'available' women.

To Ernie it was all new and exciting. He was relatively well off. After two years service and with extra pay for competence in shooting and signalling he was drawing about a hundred and twenty francs a week as compared to the French soldiers seven, and he was able to take advantage of the wonderful bread and cakes being offered for sale on the dockside. It was, he says, a similar situation to when the Yanks first landed in England. They had money to burn! They only stayed one night in Cherbourg but he made full use of it. He had his hair cut at a civilian barber's, offering a one hundred franc note in payment. When the barber objected Ernie thought it was because it was too little, whereas in reality the poor man hadn't enough money to change it!

The troops marched on from Cherbourg across France to Lannoy near Lille on the Belgian border. They took a week, averaging thirty to forty miles a day and staying the night in billets, barns and stables organised by officers who went on ahead. Again Ernie enjoyed it, revelling in the sights and sounds of the countryside and the home-baked bread and farm-churned butter. One beautiful moonlight night he and his mates went out for a drink. On their way home they passed a huge orchard and climbed over the wall to help themselves to pears. An old man with a snow-white beard was sleeping on the balcony of the house, but the noise woke him. Sitting up he saw the soldiers and thought the house was being invaded. He'd fought in the '14-'18 war and still had nightmares about it. Of course he couldn't understand the soldiers and they couldn't make out what he was trying to say, so they fled. Next day an officer who had been with them called on him to apologise and took him a peace-offering.

As they marched across France the British army was given a marvellous reception, the villagers turning out in force to clap and cheer, but many of the old folk were in tears. "You're just like your fathers," they said. "Same rifles, same puttees, same looks - just twenty years later." They realised what they were letting themselves in for. It was the same old enemy, the one they had all fought against - and many died because of - last time around. But it all meant nothing to the youngsters. Here was here and now was now. They were just anxious to get on with it.

Lannoy was just two miles from the Belgian border and across that line neutral Belgium was lit up every night, in stark contrast to the darkened countryside of France. The peasants of the Lannoy region were very poor, but they were marvellous hosts to the foreign soldiers. Part of the welcome was undoubtedly due to the money spent so freely in the cafés where steak, egg and chips cost the equivalent of two shillings. Ernie had certainly never eaten so well. There were twelve hundred and fifty men in the battalion, so the potential income was enormous. (A modern battalion is only five hundred strong).

There were of course many other battalions marching hundreds of miles back and forth across the countryside, but Monty warned that however fit they thought they were they were soft compared with the German troops whose average was fifty miles a day and whose training was much more vigorous. But his views were scoffed at and his advice ignored, the powers that be preferring to rely on their supposedly superior mechanisation. The battalion spent eight months on the border, building blockhouses and digging trenches, a period remembered by Ernie as 'sheer heaven'. 1940 was however one of the worst winters of the war as far as weather was concerned and it was in that January that Ernie was given leave and travelled home to get engaged and take Doris on the infamous trip to Beverley.

While he was in the army Ernie wrote to Doris every day, returning the loyalty she had already shown to him. In 1938, soon after they met, Chamberlain had flown to Munich and the Guards were 'stood to.' Scarlet tunics and bearskins were handed in, battledress and ammunition issued and the regiment prepared to fly from Croydon to Czechoslovakia. One hundred troop planes were on standby ready to fly to help the Czechs but Chamberlain signed the infamous 'peace treaty' and the emergency was over - at least temporarily. During this period however the Guards were confined to barracks, and Doris, anxious to know why he hadn't been to see her, went to find him. She asked the picket sentry outside the barracks if she could see him and a soldier was dispatched to seek him out. The Guards were allowed to take visitors into the library and Ernie was just conducting Doris across the pitch-dark square when a voice thundered, "Come here that man!" It was, inevitably, RSM 'Tibby' Brittain. Ernie ran over and 'pulled his tabs in', that is, came to attention. "Your great-coat's undone at the back. Take a pace to the rear and fasten the button." That done he ordered, "Right turn and carry on spit-swapping," the colloquial expression for a kiss and a cuddle! Brittain's nick-name for Ernie was 'Teal we meet again.'

Returning to France from his eventful January leave with the faithful Doris, now his official fiancee, Ernie settled down once more to enjoy the local food and drink. He was especially fond of the lemonade and would pop in to the café most mornings for a glass of this refreshing liquid and an egg sandwich. He had an army-issue bicycle which he used to take messages from battalion headquarters to all the different companies scattered along the border. As he pedalled on his way he would wave to all the local farmers and soon got to know many of them. He taught himself French, picking it up very quickly, which helped enormously. Very few of his compatriots actually bothered to learn the local language, even the officers who were of the opinion that the French should learn English if they wanted to communicate. According to Ernie most of his fellow soldiers went about like a flock of sheep, boozing and whoring and bragging about how many women they'd 'got to know', but they didn't mix with the 'ordinary' people like Ernie did, and they couldn't go back now and still find friends as Ernie has done.

One day as he was digging a trench outside Lannoy a small boy came to him and gave him an envelope containing a little cross on a chain and a note which said, "My mother give you this to keep you safe during the war." The woman in question was standing in her cottage doorway nodding and smiling. Ernie went across to her and said, "Did you give me this?" She nodded again and put her hand under his chin, lifting his face to the light. "I see you are but a child," she said. "The English always send their children. They did last time." Ernie was just twenty.

In May 1940 Ernie again went home on leave. On the day he rejoined the regiment Germany invaded Belgium, Holland and France in force. The British troops did exactly what Hitler expected them to do - they left their well-prepared positions and marched into Belgium to confront the advancing enemy. After months of relative inactivity they were spoiling for a fight. But the Germans divided and came round each side of the British troops in a pincer movement.

The first head-on encounter was at Louvain, twenty miles north of Brussels, and resulted in a Battle Honour for both the Coldstream and Grenadier Guards. They had met opposition right from the start when the Belgians had tried to stop them crossing the frontier. Now, as they travelled through Belgium in trucks they were continuously strafed by the Stukas of the German Luftwaffe. They had never seen planes like this before. The RAF were blamed for not opposing them, but they simply did not have enough aircraft to cope. Wherever they went there always seemed to be three to four hundred Stukas waiting for them, flying over the convoys all day long.

The young Guardsmen had never encountered anything like this before. The noise alone terrified them. Mostly they only had one machine-gun per lorry with which to try to retaliate. With hindsight Ernie thinks that they should have adopted the tactics employed by the Germans when attacked by the RAF in Normandy. Instead of taking cover they stood and fired with their rifles at the diving plants. A hundred rifles firing at one plane can do quite a bit of damage.

To add to the difficulties of the British troops the roads were blocked with thousands of refugees fleeing from the advancing Germans. Although Ernie never witnessed deliberate attacks on these civilians there were inevitably many casualties as the Stukas continued to harass the British troops, causing panic among the horse-drawn carts piled high with furniture and children. In the villages the attitude of the Belgians to the British was in stark contrast to the French, resentment and hostility being evident wherever they went.

When the British troops eventually arrived in the city of Louvain it had already been heavily bombed. Montgomery was with them, as was their Commanding Officer, Colonel Cazenove, father of actor Christopher and a veteran of the '14-'18 war. During their eight-month stay in Lannoy he had been in the habit of taking anyone who wanted to go out into the battlefields of the First World War to see where men of the regiment had won Victoria Crosses. Colonel Cazenove was the only one in the battalion of twelve hundred and fifty men who had been under fire. He was a big handsome man in his mid-fifties with an iron-grey moustache and was an inspiration to many of the young recruits.

Once in Louvain they were told that columns of German troops were advancing towards them. What they didn't know was that the colunms stretched back four-hundred and fifty miles into Germany and that that was just the part of the army advancing on them, never mind the other flanks. Behind the infantry were the Panzer divisions - the infantry were merely to 'break the crust'.

As the inexperienced British troops saw the enemy approaching across the field they were ordered to fix bayonets and counter-attack. With shells already dropping amongst them they were terrified. No amount of training could have prepared them for this. Several soldiers in front of Ernie started running towards the German lines. Pieces of uniform started to fly past his head as they were shot to pieces. Machine-gun bullets were going straight through them. Ernie and his comrades dropped to the ground but Lord Frederick Cambridge pulled out his revolver and shouting "The Germans are more afraid of us than we are of them," he rushed forward. He was killed instantly as were most of the battalion's best officers. The remaining troops, without adequate leadership, withdrew, ignoring the desperate whistled commands of the Commanding Officer. There was no way they were prepared to just stand there and be killed. Manoeuvres had been fun - bang, you're dead - this was quite different. This was for real, and this was hell. It was total chaos, with no semblance of sense in remaining as wounded men screamed for help and the hail of bullets flew unceasing.

Despite Montgomery's determination to hold Louvain he was ordered by Gort to withdraw through Belgium back into France. The German army had already advanced on either side and as the British marched back through Brussels the hostility of the Belgians was even more apparent, as they threw missiles and booed the weary men. They even refused to supply them with drinking water for the wounded. Ernie didn't really blame them. No longer neutral it was in their interests to be on the side of the winners. White sheets were hung from windows as the country surrendered wholesale. Ernie found it unnerving, adding to the horrors of being shelled every night wherever they stopped.

As Belgium officially capitulated the British were left to battle on alone. As they drew nearere to the French border they realised that they were lost. They saw a sign for Nieuwpoort, which is in fact near the border between Ostend and Dunkirk, but without officers they were uncertain what to do or where to head for. Just then a big staff car drew up and a British General got out. "Are you Guardsmen?" he asked and on being told yes said, "Just the chaps." He introduced a young artillery officer who, he said, would be put in charge of them.

He took them to a bridge over a canal in Nieuwpoort and told them to guard it. He advised them that they wouldn't be able to take on the big tanks, so to let them go over and then attack the baby ones! Ernie and his companions looked at each other in disbelief. When the General had left the artillery officer - 'a grand little fellow' - weighed up the situation and sent four or five of them down to the bridge to dig a slit-trench. The rest, including Ernie, were installed in a house and told to take it in turns to watch out of the window, keeping a look-out for tanks approaching the bridge. One of Ernie's friends, Jack Carron, dug-in by the bridge some thirty yards from the house with an anti-tank rifle, totally inadequate against the German vehicles. A short while later a big tank approached the bridge and, obeying orders, it was allowed to cross. It stopped and an officer in a black uniform got out. Speaking in French he offered cigarettes to the startled British and asked who they were. On being told 'Coldstream Guards' he said, "Ah yes - from Buckingham Palace." No-one else emerged from the tank although they could see machine-guns at the ready, and the officer re-mounted, the tank turned round and went back over the bridge. Only after the war, reading accounts of the battles, did they realise that the tank had been a German one, probably as lost as they were, and realising almost too late that it had crossed into forbidden territory.

In a field near the bridge was a crashed German bomber and after some time with no further activity Ernie went to have a look at it. It still had its quota of bombs on board and a soldier from a different regiment came running up and told Ernie to get away as the Navy were about to blow it up. Ernie was bewildered - they had no idea that they were so close to the sea. He ran back to the house very shaken, and retired to the cellar. There he found a man dressed in grey trousers and shirt and jackboots. "Who are you?" asked Ernie. "Belgique," he was told, but later realised that he must have been one of the German air-crew from the crashed bomber.

At the time however he had no chance to pursue enquiries as the Artillery Officer shouted, "Come up here all of you - quick." Six German soldiers were advancing across the field on the other side of the canal, crawling towards the bridge. "Engage the enemy," the officer commanded. Ernie was terrified. It was the first time he had had to fire at the Germans at close range. He just pointed his rifle in the general direction of the enemy and fired! They turned and fled behind a small brick building with a chimney. Encouraged by his success Ernie regained his composure. "I'll let you know I can shoot," he muttered, adjusted his sights and started taking pot-shots at the chimney. That was where his lack of experience let him down, because it pinpointed their position. At that moment he swears he heard his mother's voice telling him to 'get out of here'. He ran down to the cellar just as the first shell hit the house. The whole house collapsed above him as he shared his refuge with the German airman.

When the shelling stopped he was, miraculously, able to climb out of the rubble. A dispatch rider who had come to tell them to abandon their position had been blown to pieces. In the confusion Ernie's friend Jack Carron, in the slit trench by the bridge, not realising that there were any Germans on the other side of the canal and assuming that the house had been taken by the enemy started returning his companion's fire. With German soldiers rushing towards the bridge the remaining twenty Guardsmen retreated, dodging over garden walls and fences to avoid the enemy fire. A civilian who spoke good English told them the Germans were everywhere and that they should make their way to Dunkirk, where the British were being evacuated. Ernie and his companions were suspicious. They'd heard all about fifth columnists spreading rumours of defeat and leading unwary soldiers into traps. A Sergeant Quarmley accompanied by a Guardsman went to try and find out was happening. After three hours he came back with the terrible news that they were indeed taking the British off. It was May 31st. 1940.

# Chapter 7

## THE LULL BEFORE THE STORM

By the time Ernie and his small band reached Dunkirk they were reduced to ten men. They arrived to a scene of chaos and devastation. Stukas were dive-bombing and machine-gunning the retreating Allied troops as boats of all shapes and sizes evacuated them from the beaches. An officer of a line-regiment approached them and asked them to call out their names as he needed someone to go back up the beach to keep watch for the advancing Germans. Ernie was just congratulating himself on being well down the order with the initial 'T' when the officer took them in reverse and he found himself up over the dunes with the only shelter being a very small tree. He clutched the trunk as another wave of several hundred Stukas came over, so low that he could see the fair hair of one pilot under his helmet. He took a pot shot at him with his rifle - a useless gesture, but it made him feel better. He was shaking with fear to such an extent that the leaves fell from the tree.

At nightfall he returned to the beach, where the chaos and panic had worsened. Officers were doing their best to restore some sort of order, even threatening to shoot soldiers trying to jump the queues for the boats. Ernie and five companions decided to move further along the coast to a cove called La Panne. They had to pick their way through hundreds of dead bodies and as they did so they saw an Adjutant calling for Coldstreamers to rally to him. Jack Carron and Tug Wilson, two old soldiers in Ernie's group, warned him to ignore the call, as it would be for a last - and obviously hopeless - stand against the advancing enemy. As he spoke a German shell landed on the Adjutant and the Guards who had run towards him, killing them outright.

Ernie and his companions carried on along the beach and at 2.00am saw a cruiser out in the bay signalling 'Any more British soldiers?' Ernie had hung on to his signalling lamp throughout the retreat so sent back the cryptic message 'six' - all that now remained of the twenty who had escaped from the siege at the bridge. A rowing boat put off from the cruiser and with agonising slowness came towards them. It was manned by exhausted young sailors who had been ferrying troops back and forth all night. The soldiers waded out and were hauled aboard, but Ernie's gas mask caught on a rowlock and as the boat set off into deep water he was dragged under. One of the sailors jumped over the side and hoisted him in.

As they approached the cruiser the Captain was leaning over the rail yelling at them to get alongside as it would soon be daylight, but the exhausted sailors had great difficulty in manoeuvring the overloaded boat into position. They were further hampered by the bodies floating in the water. A huge explosion lit up the sky as a nearby destroyer suffered a direct hit highlighting the urgency of immediate withdrawal. Eventually they tied up and a rope ladder was thrown down the side. In his haste to climb to safety Ernie moved too quickly and found his fingers being trodden on by the man above him, but it was a small price to pay for cheating death for the umpteenth time.

Once on board they were taken down to the engine-room where they fell into an exhausted sleep. They were woken at intervals by the fires burning on stricken vessels in the channel and finally by a sailor shaking them awake to tell they they had arrived in Dover. Still half-asleep and stupid with weariness they shuffled off the ship, defeated and demoralised. The unthinkable had happened - they had been beaten and driven back to England by the hated German army.

As they assembled on the dockside in a dejected huddle they heard a familiar voice. RSM Brittain was there to greet them - but if they expected sympathy they were disappointed. The great booming voice berated them for running away, for their shambolic appearance and for their dejection. He marched them up and down the quay, back and forth until they once again bore some resemblance to 'his' Guards. Then he marched them to the train and waved them off. They were heading for Porthcawl in Wales and at every station they were met by civilians offering them drinks, cakes and biscuits from their meagre rations, and asking them if they wanted their field-cards posting to relatives. Ernie gratefully wrote one to Doris - it said quite simply 'Safe in England!' Doris still has it, safely stored away with many of the thousand and more letters he wrote to her during their six-year separation.

They arrived at Porthcawl at midnight and it soon became clear that the Guards had suffered terrible losses. There were only about a hundred and twenty left out of the battalion of twelve hundred and fifty Coldstreamers and a pitiful twenty-seven from the Grenadiers.

As they disembarked in the Square at Porthcawl they were greeted by the Mayor and most of the inhabitants, who each took two or three soldiers into their homes. A miner and his wife took Ernie in, fed him and gave him a bath in front of the fire. The only thing that bothered him in his stupefied state was that they took his rifle away - he had kept it with him throughout the conflict and the remnants of long-instilled discipline told him he shouldn't let go of it.

He remained in Porthcawl for a fortnight, palling up with a soldier from the Royal Corps of Signals and they went for long walks along the beach as they waited for their Regiments to re-form. The local population was very good to them, despite the poverty affecting the region and the rationing. Ernie vividly remembers with gratitude and pleasure the apple pies and custard served up on Sundays.

Eventually he was ordered to report back to camp in Poole in Dorset on the south coast. He stayed there six months, building scaffolding right across Studland Bay. It had been reported that enemy sea-planes had been landing there to drop agents. Other reports said that to boost morale bodies - victims of the blitz - were being brought from London, dressed in German uniforms and laid on the beach to simulate a repulsed invasion. Announcements were made about 'Operation Sealion', in which RAF bombers were said to have sunk barge-loads of German troops. The Royal Engineers assisted in the laying of mines along the coast, watching as they did so the waves of enemy bombers coming over in daylight to bomb London. It was altogether a bad time.

From Poole Ernie was sent to Midsomer Norton in Somerset - a delightful place with which he instantly fell in love. He was again billeted with a mining family who lived next door to a dairy and again fed on apple pie and custard, for which he retains a particular fondness. He made friends with the manageress of the local Co-op, 'a bonny dark-haired lass' called Olive Lambourne who came from Bath.

The port of Bristol was being heavily bombed by the Germans at that time and many of the planes were shot down. If the crews baled out it was one of the duties of the Guards to go and pick them up. Ernie remembers one airman in particular who was small and dark and spoke good English. He was bothered about missing a date with his girl-friend in France, but was told in no uncertain manner that he'd be missing her for a long time to come. He was however full of confidence that the Führer would come and liberate them within a few days. His confidence was dented when he asked about his co-pilot and was taken to see his body. His parachute hadn't opened and he had landed on the road.

In August 1941 the invasion scare was at its height. Ernie was worried about Doris. The army wasn't particularly short of food but he knew rationing was biting hard amongst the civilians and that the bombing was becoming more severe. The troops were moved inland to avoid the coastal bombardment and regrouped ready to repel invaders. Regiments of regular soldiers were retained in England as a last line of defence, while conscripts and Territorials went abroad, particularly to the Middle East. Several times the Guards were issued with Middle East gear, but each time the orders were rescinded. A Canadian Division was also held back to help out in the bomb-devastated cities.

The King expressed a personal wish for the Guards remaining in Britain to be re-formed into an armoured division. They had always traditionally been infantry regiments, armed with rifles and bayonets. Now they were to be issued with tanks. They were sent to Tidworth in Hampshire for three months intensive training. Unfortunately this didn't initially coincide with the arrival of the Crusaders and they had to run around with their arms out pretending to be tanks. For a bunch of high-spirited nineteen and twenty-year olds this was great fun. The local population thought they'd gone mad!

In September 1941 Ernie was given ten days leave to get married. After the ceremony in Beverley Minster he and Doris spent their honeymoon at his beloved Granny Railton's in Norton Street, spending much of their time walking on Beverley Westwood. They carved their names on a tree in Union Bushes, and they can still take you to it after more than fifty years. Reluctant to leave his bride Ernie reported back to his regiment in Longbridge Deverill in Wiltshire twenty four hours late. He had already been posted 'Absent Without Leave' and was arrested as soon as he arrived in camp and marched in front of the Earl of Denby, his Company Commander. Ernie offered his marriage as an excuse adding that he didn't expect him to understand. "On the contrary," he was told, "I got married at the same time, but I had to be back promptly." However, Ernie was lucky, he was let off with a severe reprimand instead of the fourteen days 'jankers' he'd been expecting.

Longbridge Deverill was, as far as Ernie was concerned, heaven on earth. On his next leave he collected Doris from her parents' home in London and they travelled up to stay with his parents in Beverley. His dad had a pole-cat ferret called Felix and Ernie took it back with him to camp. His long-time mate was Jack Carron of the 3rd Battalion. Jack had served in Palestine and was really tough, a dangerous exponent of unarmed combat and with an evil temper. He was also a cook and he and Ernie soon created a thriving business out of rabbiting.

Jack already had a ferret called Esmeraldo and they 'acquired' two terriers called Jack and Peter. Soon Ernie was able to send three or four couples of rabbits a week to Doris and his family by post. After he had gutted and cleaned them he would pack them with currants and raisins from Jack's stores. Surplus rabbits were sold to the cooks from the Sergeants' Mess, who in turn prepared and cooked them and sold them on to the Officers' Mess as chicken! Ernie and Jack were making about ten pounds a week each - an enormous amount in those days - and a very acceptable supplement to Doris's meagre income.

One moonlight night Jack was on duty and couldn't accompany Ernie, so he went alone taking both ferrets and dogs. It was a beautiful night, clear and frosty and he was busily digging out a burrow in a clearing in the wood when one of the terriers started to growl. His hackles were up, and Ernie stopped digging and rose cautiously to his feet. A big man with a gun walked out of the trees carrying a pheasant. At first Ernie thought he was a keeper, but then noticed the flat army cap and as he came forward into the moonlight recognised him as his Commanding Officer, Major Anstruther-Gray. He greeted him with, "Now then Teal, how are you doing?" "Oh - I've got a few rabbits Sir. How about you?" "Not bad - got one and winged another. Carry on," and he strolled off into the wood.

The woods they were poaching were part of the Longleat Estate belonging to the Marquis of Bath and now of course famous for its Safari Park. One Saturday afternoon when Ernie and Jack were doing the rounds of the traps they'd set the previous night they bumped into one of his Lordship's keepers, who threatened them with prosecution. Jack Carron was totally unimpressed and threatened in turn to blow the keeper's head off. The keeper wisely retreated.

When Jack was on leave Ernie used to take another mate - a Geordie - with him on his poaching trips. One winter's day when the going was particularly heavy after rain they were struggling back to camp loaded down with some twenty rabbits each plus their 4.10's, ferrets and dogs. They had one more ploughed field to cross before reaching the safety of the camp perimeter but the gate was locked and they had to scramble through the side. Geordie declared that he couldn't carry the rabbits any further, Ernie said in that case he wouldn't get any of the profits, but Geordie was exhausted, dumped his burden and made his own way back. Ernie struggled on alone and on his return immediately sold most of his booty. He took the remaining six rabbits into his barrack-room. By now he was running late. He had a leather sack in which he kept his ferrets, so he stowed them in his locker, the rabbits in his kit-bag, his gun in his bed and the dogs underneath it, deciding to deal with them after tea. Suddenly whistles blew, a Sergeant appeared at either end of the hut and the Company Commander walked in with the Sergeant Major. They were ordered to 'stand by their beds'. A recruit had had five pounds stolen from his locker and everyone was being searched.

As an 'old soldier' and a Guardsman Ernie's bed was nearest the door, so he was searched first. Included in the contents of his pockets as he turned them out were several very second-hand sausages. He explained that they were for feeding the stray dogs which hung around the camp. "Good man," said the Earl. "Good-hearted chap." However when his kit-bag was tipped out to reveal half-a-dozen rabbits and his locker yielded up two ferrets he wasn't so complimentary and the revelation of the 4.10 in and the two terriers under the bed was the last straw. "Teal," he was told, "you're either a conjurer or a poacher. Whichever, you're contravening goodness knows how many rules and regulations. You're under arrest." Ernie was 'fell in' between two Guardsmen and quick-marched in the direction of the 'clink'.

After about thirty yards a command rang out, "Halt escort," followed by,

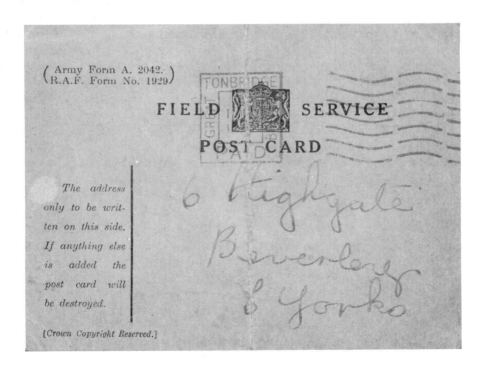

*Field Service postcard, sent to Doris after Dunkirk.*

NOTHING is to be written on this side except the date and signature of the sender. Sentences not required may be erased. If anything else is added the post card will be destroyed.

[Postage must be prepaid on any letter or post card addressed to the sender of this card.]

I am quite well.

I have been admitted into hospital
{ sick } and am going on well.
{ wounded } and hope to be discharged soon.

I am being sent down to the base.

I have received your { letter dated
{ telegram ,,
{ parcel ,,

Letter follows at first opportunity.

I have received no letter from you
{ lately
{ for a long time.

Signature only

Date

Forms/A2042/7.    51-4997.

(Army Form A. 2042.)
(R.A.F. Form No. 1929)

FIELD SERVICE POST CARD

The address only to be written on this side. If anything else is added the post card will be destroyed.

[Crown Copyright Reserved.]

6 Highgate
Beverley
E Yorks

"Dismiss escort." Lord Denby confronted Ernie and said he thought he'd better speak to him personally. He said he wasn't against poaching as such, it was good training for the conflict to come, but there were one or two matters that had to be cleared up. For example, how did he feed the ferrets and the dogs? Ernie went into a complicated explanation about draining the dregs from discarded milk tins and collecting waste scraps only to be told he was a liar. 'Don't add lying to poaching' was the advice he got. He was told to house the dogs and ferrets in a spare Nissen hut and warned about selling rabbits to the Sergeants' Mess, as the entrepreneurial cook there had also been rumbled. Sir William had apparently regaled his fellow officers with his story of meeting Ernie by moonlight and the ample supplies of 'chicken' had immediately come under suspicion! Yet again, however, Ernie was let off with a caution and merely curtailed his poaching expeditions accordingly.

It was while he was stationed at Longbridge Deverill that Doris visited him and was billeted with a Mrs Shepherd and her daughter in a picture-postcard thatched cottage in the village. She was introduced to the infamous Jack Carron and his wife. Jack was a Cumberland man, given to shouting at his wife, and he used to frighten Doris. In his late thirty's and having seen active service in Palestine he used to brag about how many men he'd killed. Doris used to be able to visit for as much as a fortnight at a time - a welcome relief from the blitz.

Meanwhile, Ernie was learning to drive. He admits that he never became a very good driver, and in fact has never owned either a civilian licence or a car. The attraction was the extra three shillings and sixpence a day added to your pay packet after you passed the test. He practised at first on thirty-hundredweight and three-ton lorries, with a Captain instructor. There were ten in his group and as well as learning to drive they had to be able to carry out all the other duties of a tank - crew commander, gunner, wireless operator, gun-loader - in case any were killed in action.

The day after Ernie's first long drive they were gathered together to hear how they were getting on. An officer (Ernie can't remember precisely who - 'the Honourable something - a big shot,') said, "There's a man here who is quite heavy-handed. I'm not going to say who it is until he offends again, then I'm going to give him a right bollocking."

They set off for a test drive in the Crusaders and when it got down to the last two or three without an outburst Ernie began to speculate on who it could be. Then it was his turn. "Right Teal - off we go. Up into second - right, change gear. *Change gear!*"

Thwack. The officer's riding crop came down across his knuckles. The tank zig-zagged wildly as Ernie sucked his bruised hand. "Yes Teal, it's you, this gear lever is bent. You bent it yesterday. I've told you - treat it like a woman - gently - along the corridor and upstairs to bed. Not bang! without any thought at all. Now - let's do a hill start."

Eventually Ernie did pass his test, but it took a long time. Once in exasperation his instructor berated him with, "I'll tell you something. There are convoys crossing the Atlantic facing submarines and planes and there are men fighting overseas in ghastly conditions just to bring petrol for idiots like you to learn to drive."

Despite his limited driving abilities Ernie has been promoted to Sergeant by the time he finally took his test in a Sherman tank. His co-driver on the fateful day was George Denham, and he gave Ernie some sound advice. "Right Duke," (Ernie's nick-name in the battalion) "We're going into the centre of Warminster and it will be busy.

When he makes you reverse keep your foot off the accelerator altogether. Just let it idle back. That way you'll be in control."

They arrived in the square in Warminster without mishap and he was told to turn round and go back the way he'd come. He was so relieved he forgot the advice, put it into reverse, foot on the accelerator and zoomed back to horrified shouts of, "Stop - stop." He did but not before he had pinned a man on a motor-bike up against a wall with the tank-tracks inches from his face. "Switch off for God's sake while I go and talk to the unfortunate victim." Ernie thought he'd crushed him to death.

After Longbridge Deverill he was sent to Sheffield where there was a 'live ammo' range. In the evenings they ran a three-ton truck (known as the 'Passion Wagon') into the city centre for off-duty troops. One of the lads - 'Cooper CR' - actually lived in Sheffield, and invited Ernie to accompany him home for a meal. Ernie was in charge of the party and the driver was 'Nipper' Lake. He instructed everyone to be back at the rendezvous by 11.00pm and went off to enjoy Mrs. Cooper's hospitality which included a supper of scalloped potatoes and eggs. At the appointed time they returned to the truck to find thirty inebriated soldiers, including the driver. Nipper assured them he would be all right once he got behind the wheel. Just then the siren sounded the alert. In total blackout and on unfamiliar roads they set off.

In the dimmed headlights Ernie could just make out a warning sign ahead of them but before he could read what it said an electricity pylon loomed out of the darkness. They hit it head on and Ernie was catapulted through the windscreen and slid down the bonnet to the ground. Everyone was eventually taken to the local hospital with a variety of injuries including fractures, only half a dozen being fit enough not to be detained overnight.

Ernie miraculously escaped with only bruised knees and rang for another truck to take the walking wounded back to camp. The RASC were based in Sheffield and they sent a vehicle to pick them up at the hospital. They all piled in but on the way back they were flagged down by two Grenadiers who sat on the tailboard. Unbelievably this truck also crashed and the Grenadiers flew down the interior like bowls in an alley, felling the survivors like ninepins. Back they all went to hospital.

When Ernie eventually returned to camp the Commanding Officer 'went mad'. Next day they went to view the three-tonner which was still wrapped round the pylon with a huge light swinging above it on a single chain. The other three supporting chains had been snapped by the impact. Ernie could dimly remember after the crash that a girl had been leaning over him asking him how to switch off the petrol which was dripping from the truck's engine but he was in no fit state to tell her even if he had known. If the light *had* fallen there would obviously have been an almighty explosion. Yet again Ernie had had a miraculous escape.

His next posting was to Brandon in Norfolk, equipped with Sherman tanks. He loved it there because of the wildlife. They were surrounded by forests used by Bryant and May as a source of timber for matches. This time they were housed in tents. It was an easy although strictly forbidden journey to London. They used to catch the train ostensibly for Salisbury and on the way back jump out before it stopped to avoid both the ticket collectors and the Military Police.

One Sunday night they arrived to find the station surrounded by hundreds of Redcaps and Snowdrops - British and American MP's. They piled out of the train in a panic and galloped off in all directions. One soldier caught his foot in a fire bucket as he tried to climb the fence and was felled by a Snowdrop. They were quite formidable in their white helmets and gaiters, armed with what Ernie describes as 'pick-shafts wrapped in lead'.

He, as usual, escaped and was making his way back to base with the other lucky ones when they were overtaken by a convoy of about a hundred Canadian tanks manned by French Canadians. They asked the way to their camp and Ernie was about to tell them when his more canny mate nudged him and said 'it was a bit complicated'. They could however show them he added. They jumped on the leading tank and started directing them in the direction of their own camp but about half a mile from the gates they jumped off and melted into the trees. When they arrived back they could hear the commotion as the Canadians ran through the camp looking for them but managed to lie low until the hubub died down.

It was at Brandon that two local girls were 'put in the family way' and a complaint was made by their parents. The Commanding Officer called all the troops out on parade, explained the situation and asked the guilty men to step forward. They did - to a man!

From Brandon Ernie went to Duncombe Park near Helmsley, former seat of the Earls of Feversham but since 1930 a girls' school. It was a 'good spot' not far from home. The Guards were stationed there because Intelligence sources said German Paratroops were to be dropped on the Yorkshire Moors. It was a pointless exercise but Ernie took the opportunity to rustle a few sheep which were butchered by the camp cook, parcelled up and sent home. Then after a spell back in the south west of the country near Bath they were on the move again, this time to an unknown destination.

They travelled all night by train and when they stopped he put his head out of the window to find they were just four miles south of Driffield. In great excitement he shook his sleeping mates. "Wake up - we're in God's Own Country."

They were stationed in tents on part of the Sledmere Estate at Butterwick and it was there that Churchill came to talk to them. Five or six battalions and their tanks were lined up as he climbed into a pristine White's armoured car to tour the ranks. Unfortunately it wouldn't start and he had to transfer to an extremely dirty one to drive along the lines.

He addressed them over the loudspeakers saying that they must be fed up with sleeping with other peoples' wives but that soon they would be going into battle, which they would win, then they could all go home. He added that they were the first to be told the good news that when they were demobilised they would all be given sixpence (two and a half new pence) for every day they had served in the army, in order to give them a good start in civvy street. Everybody cheered like mad. Such generosity.

What it actually amounted to was nine pounds two shillings and sixpence per year or less than fifty pounds after five years of fighting. But on that summer evening in 1943 who cared? The war would soon be over. Churchill said so.

# Chapter 8

## THE LONG WAY BACK

The pace of Ernie's war was hotting up, but before he left Sledmere he forged yet another of those enduring friendships which have been a feature of his whole life. He as usual made a habit of walking around the countryside whenever he was able and one evening, coming across a farmer stooking corn, offered his help. As they chatted they exchanged names and Ernie told him he came from Beverley. Horace Woodhall invited him home to meet his wife Ethel and his twin sons. They were talking in the farmyard when an old cockerel attacked the little boys and swearing and cursing Horace said he'd done it once too often and that he was going to ring its neck, take its jacket off and put it in the pot!

Forty-four years later Ernie was giving a talk at Foston-on-the-Wolds and told the story about Horace and the cockerel. To his amazement Horace and Ethel still lived in the district. They had sold the farm for a good price and had a bungalow built, just down the road from the village hall. Ernie and Doris and their driver, Dick Pinder, went and knocked on the door. "Now then Mr. Woodhall, do you remember me?" asked Ernie, but Horace didn't. "See yon cock-bird," said Ernie, "I'm going to ring its neck for dinner." Horace looked at him as if he'd gone made, but when he added, "You've done it once too often to them lads," light dawned. "Now 'od 'ard a bit. You're never Ernie Teal are you?" After that of course the excitement was great. Ethel was 'next door' baby-sitting in a big house built on land sold to the owner by Horace.

When he went to fetch his wife he told her that some people had come to the bungalow after their car had broken down and that he'd offered them a meal and a bed for the night. She was quite naturally a bit flustered and pushed past her guests without really looking at them, saying she'd better 'get the beds fettled'! "Don't you know me Ethel?" Ernie asked, but yet again he went unrecognised. It wasn't surprising. The last time they'd seen him he'd been a young soldier in his early twenties and although he had written to them after he left they had subsequently heard that he'd been killed. Ethel disappeared upstairs and came back with his letter, written in Normandy and carefully preserved.

While he was stationed at Sledmere, Doris, by then pregnant and back with her parents in London, used to travel up to see Ernie as often as she could. She had got a job in London making army uniforms but gave that up when she was expecting their first baby, due in February 1944. By then Ernie was back down south, but before the battalion left the north there was one more pointless exercise to be conducted. Code-named Exercise Spartan it was to take place on February 12th when the troops, based at Helmsley, were to be landed at Robin Hoods Bay from infantry and tank landing craft in freezing cold weather with very limited access. It was not a success!

Back in the south of England Ernie had his first experience of Flying Bombs. With talk of the Allied Invasion of Europe in the air Hitler was desperately trying to destroy the preparing troops. The first 'doodle-bug' he saw landed on a massive commercial greenhouse just outside Brighton, causing havoc from flying glass. He was stationed at Hove, a suburb of Brighton which was cut off by barbed wire, only authorised residents and workers being allowed in. There were miles and miles of ammunition dumps in Nissen huts alongside all the roads. Brigadier Barker's wife who lived locally used to invite batches of troops to the house in the evening to play table-tennis and drink coffee and tea. All the residents were very kind and Ernie kept in touch with many of them.

During February Ernie became a father for the first time. Doris was evacuated from London to Ruskin College, Oxford, for the birth. In later life Christine was to say it was the nearest she ever got to University! Doris and baby Christine stayed there for a fortnight and Ernie was given leave to visit them. Christine was wrapped tightly in a blanket - the custom with new babies in those days - and in Ernie's opinion looked like 'a dumpling in a hankie'. Doris still tuts over his comments to this day. "Fancy saying that about his own daughter," she says. From Oxford Ernie returned to camp and Doris to London to live again with her parents, as they had no money to rent or buy a home of their own even if one had been available. "Nobody realises if they didn't live through those years how much was missing from life," says Doris. Living with parents inevitably created friction on both sides. Ernie didn't see his daughter for over a year. She was three months old when he sailed for France after D-Day and eighteen months by the time he returned.

In conversation with his Dad Ernie had speculated that D-Day would be on June 5th. He would have been right if it hadn't been for the weather! Their first inkling that the invasion had begun was when they saw wave after wave of planes flying over with black and white stripes painted on their under-sides for identification. They had been trained in landing techniques on the beaches at Littlehampton and as a Sergeant Ernie had been to Scotland to learn how to waterproof his tank. A chute was fitted to the exhaust to keep it clear of the water, then the entire vehicle was sealed inside a waterproof skin. This meant that the tank could be submerged in up to ten feet of water, with only the exhaust chute emerging from the surface. Once on dry land the tank driver plugged a lead into the dashboard and the waterproofing was literally blown off. Every nut and bolt was dipped in grease to keep it dry and in theory the method was foolproof as well as waterproof. In theory!

The Coldstreams embarked from Gosport heading for Arromanches. They were transported across the channel on American landing craft which was a mixed blessing. The food was superb - turkey, and roast potatoes dipped in sugar - the first time Ernie had tasted them cooked like that. But the loading of the tanks left a lot to be desired. There were queues of troops waiting to embark and there were inevitably long delays and exhortations to speed it up. Once loaded the ships had to stand off the shore until enough were ready to form a convoy. The American crew, presumably in an effort to hurry things along, didn't secure the tanks properly in the hold and during the notoriously stormy weather following D-Day the tanks came loose and started crashing backwards and forwards. The ships were 'liberty ships', built by American shipyards in the emergency, and certainly not intended for this kind of treatment. As it lurched and shuddered the Captain ordered his crew below to re-fasten the restraining chains. Ernie was glad it wasn't him - twenty unmanned thirty-two-ton Sherman tanks loose in the hold of a ship must have been a terrifying spectacle.

Another disturbing incident was the disappearance of items of their equipment. They had been issued with .38 Colt Automatics and Tommy-guns, which some of the Americans obviously saw as ideal souvenirs. Order was restored when over the Tannoy came the Captain's voice. "Now hear this you guys. These Limeys want their guns back. If they're not returned pronto there will be no shore leave." Not quite British Naval language, but effective.

As they arrived off the French coast the attacking fleet, which included the *Renown*, was bombarding the enemy position with 16" guns. They were, says Ernie, 'making a helluva din.' Many of the young soldiers hadn't been in action before and found it all quite terrifying.

As they neared the beach an American sailor with a plumb-line tested the depth constantly to make sure the ship didn't run aground before it was safe to disembark the tanks. Unfortunately his judgement was faulty. The ramp went down and the first tank with its crew sealed inside went down - and down. The water was much too deep. A stream of bubbles from the exhaust chute was the only thing to be seen and the crew died without ever firing a shot. The ramp was hauled up, the ship backed off and then went in again in a different position.

Ernie's tank was next off. They were given the signal to go, then frantic signals to stop. Halting a thirty two ton tank rolling down a steep ramp isn't easy. The driver pulled on the stick, the tank slewed and hit the water sideways. The tank rocked violently twice and they thought they were going to roll right over, but just then the tracks hit the sand and they managed to get clear. It only lasted moments, but to the five men sealed claustrophobically inside the limited space with all their equipment it seemed like a life-time. Once the waterproofing had been blown off however they could open the hatches and take stock of their surroundings.

Before embarkation, within hours of the initial landings on D-Day, the troops had been assembled in a Brighton cinema for a pep-talk. A German prisoner had been paraded before them, deliberately chosen for his small stature and they were told this was what they would be up against. The initial landing, it was asserted, had gone very well and Montgomery was well pleased.

When they actually landed they soon found that most of these statements had been at the very least optimistic. Despite a continuous bombardment up to twenty miles inland the German army where not being pushed back - they were far too well dug in. However the beach landings themselves were well organised. There were ramps for the tanks and in no time they were through Arromanches and out into the open countryside to the farmlands. The countryside itself was beautiful, but every-where was the sickening smell of death.

The pep-talks from the officers continued. After nearly five years of war England was getting short of men willing to fight and in all probability die. Many of them had been this way before and only just escaped with their lives. Exhorted by their superiors to regard it as a great crusade about which they would be able to tell their grandchildren, many of them doubted whether they would have grandchildren to tell. The only thing that did strike home, especially to Ernie as a new father, was being told that if they didn't stop the Germans now they would conquer England. They were quite literally fighting to save their wives, their families and their homes.

The French homes they were now encountering were of course being over-run for the third or fourth time and although the British troops were on the whole made welcome, they were not nearly as disciplined as the German army, who would be shot if caught raping or looting. The only non-British Regiment in Ernie's sector, the

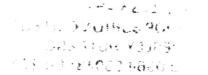

French Canadians, were even worse, treating the French civilians very badly and being quite uncontrollable, even by Montgomery.

The first attack to be mounted by the Coldstream battalion was Operation Goodwood. Prior to embarkation they had been told that the 7th and 11th Armoured Divisions and the Guards Armoured Division were to break out of the bridge-head which had been established. The 7th Armoured were the original Desert Rats, brought back to strengthen the invasion forces. Churchill had talked to them all about the plan of attack then Montgomery had reinforced his ideas and finally Eisenhower had visited them. Eisenhower intrigued Ernie, but he still put his faith in Montgomery who had a reputation for not moving forward until he was ready, however hard he was pushed by Churchill and Eisenhower.

One thing the troops were promised was that this time round the Luftwaffe would not dominate the skies. There would be none of the unopposed Stuka attacks. This time there would be so many allied planes in the sky 'even the godamned birds would have to walk.' Another supposed morale booster was being taken to see some knocked-out German tanks, but Ernie wished he hadn't gone. The sight of a sixty ton Tiger albeit with a broken track frightened him to death. It was twice the size of his Sherman! Even the Panthers at forty-five tons dwarfed them and their 88mm guns were massive. They could destroy a convoy of three Shermans at a range of a mile with one shot. The Germans called the British tanks 'Tommy-cookers' because they carried a hundred and twenty gallons of petrol which blew up if they were hit, trapping the crew inside. Their 75mm guns were like pea-shooters compared with the German armoury, the three foot high shells looking like miniatures beside those of the 88mm's.

Every Sherman carried fifty rounds of ammunition for the main gun, three Browning automatic machine guns and grenades. It was extremely crowded with two men at the controls and three in the turret. One small advantage over the Germans was the power traverse for the gun, but even this had its hazards. Big men tended to sit outside the turret which weighed five tons, and if power traversing at speed could take off a man's foot.

As Operation Goodwood got under way they were told that there were two thousand seven hundred and fifty planes in the air, heavy bombers, fighter bombers and fighters, which would turn Normandy into a lunar landscape. They would, said Monty, break the SS. Intelligence Officers brought the news that the troops opposing them were the 123rd and 124th infantry and - pause - the 10th and 12th SS. Everybody cringed. They were renowned as the finest fighting troops in the world. The Allied forces however were making progress, if slowly. They managed to establish a very narrow bridge-head. At least they had a foot-hold and had made room for more troops to be brought in.

Following the air-bombardment the three divisions were to break out. They moved half-a-mile forward, but then began what became the 'death-ride' of the armoured division. The Germans were dug in, in depth, with their 88mm guns. Colonel Middleton, the Commanding Officer, called off the attack but by then the Guards Armoured Division had lost sixty tanks and the 11th were almost wiped out. There were fifty-two tanks in a battalion and four battalions to a division and a quarter were lost in the first twenty minutes. In all seven hundred tanks were lost that day. There were some ten thousand tanks in reserve, and they could be and were

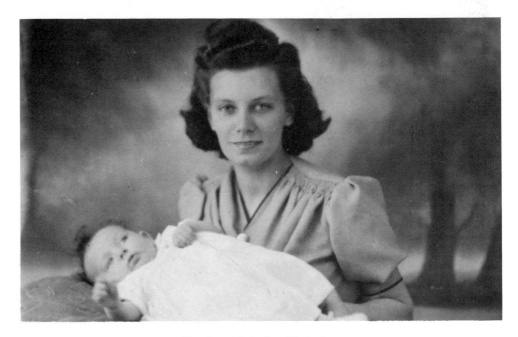

*Doris with baby Christine.*

*12 Coldstream Guards killed September 8th 1944 at Heppen in Belgium.*
*Buried here, then taken to the military cemetery at Leopoldsburg in 1945.*

*Grave of Ernie's friend, Sergeant Moffatt at Beverley,
killed at Heppen, Belgium in 1944.*

*Grave Bridge.*

*Grave of the Marquis of Hartington, who married Joan Kennedy, sister of John F. Kennedy, and who was killed at Heppen in 1944.*

*Nijmegen, September 1944. Ernie 2nd from left, with Sir William Anstruther-Gray, MC, MP (centre).*

*Ernie at Nijmegen, September 1944.*

replaced, but the men who died were irreplaceable, there were no trained crews left.

The army was shaken. They had lost confidence in their equipment. The battalion's Second in Command, Major Anstruther-Gray, was Chairman of the 1922 Back-bench Committee and he flew back to Britain to speak to the House of Commons, denouncing the Sherman tank as inadequate. Churchill and Montgomery were not pleased, saying that they had to make do with what they'd got. With ten thousand already completed they couldn't change the design, although belatedly they realised that compared with the German tanks it was a David and Goliath situation. What they did do was to replace the 75mm guns with a seventeen pounder on every fourth tank. This was capable of knocking out a Tiger - if it could get near enough! The gunners were told to aim for the hatch in the hope of stunning the driver but the Germans could open fire at a range of a mile and a half, which gave the Shermans little chance of retaliation. Then the Typhoons started firing rockets, and rockets were fitted to the sides of some tanks, which helped enormously.

Gradually, by the British drawing the armour towards them, the Americans captured Cherbourg, albeit at a frightful cost. 'Blood and guts' Patton arrived, and the Americans swung left. Patton was the one General the Germans really feared and the Yanks soon broke out of the bridge-head and the whole army high-tailed it across France to Arras, the place where they had fought a final battle against the Germans in 1940. They knocked out the anti-tank guns and pushed on, at such a speed that they inadvertently over-ran the front line and while filling up with fuel they were attacked by their own aircraft, losing both men and trucks. The tanks fared better as they were able to close down, but it was a desperate situation as they were of course ordered not to return fire.

As the Allied army advanced they became aware that despite their sophisticated weapons the German army relied heavily on horse power, having the largest collection of horse-drawn transport in the world. They commandeered fresh horses wherever they went as there were inevitably huge losses during the bombardment. The French, desperate for food, collected up the carcasses to supplement their meagre rations.

Soon the Allies' superior air-power began to tell. The continuous bombardment behind enemy lines prevented reinforcements being brought up by rail or road and the advancing ground forces came across column after column of enemy vehicles knocked out before they could reach the front. Monty called it 'a battle of attrition' an apt description as one hundred thousand German troops died in Normandy alone. Many of them were Hitler Youth serving with the German 12th SS - the pick of the German army lost in a matter of weeks. The French Resistance played their part, crawling up to the allied tanks to point out the German positions, but they paid a terrible price, many of them being summarily hung from trees. Then one night the Commanding Officer gathered the Guards together and said, "The Little Man says tomorrow you are to take Brussels." It was ninety-seven miles away and as soon as it was light they set off, not stopping until they arrived on the outskirts of the city at dusk.

The Welsh Guards led the way into Brussels. The streets were eerily quiet at first. Then the civilians realised that these were a different kind of tanks and rushed out of their houses shouting 'Les Anglais, les Anglais.' They poured out in their thousands, the lights began to go on, and the champagne began to flow. It was

September 3rd 1944 - the fifth anniversary of the outbreak of the war that was to be 'all over by Christmas'.

As they approached Brussels one of the tanks in Ernie's troop had suffered a broken track and had been left behind for repairs to be carried out. When they were completed it joined a supply column of trucks. The Tank Commander was Lt. Towers-Clarke, the driver Corporal Timbrell and the co-driver Bill Franks. The crew was completed by gunner Skid Craven and wireless operator Jimmy Trent. Suddenly half a dozen German trucks and an armoured car came out of a side-road where they had lain in wait to ambush what they thought was a 'soft' target. They were totally unprepared for the presence of the tank, which drove straight at the enemy and 'flattened the lot of them.' When they did finally arrive in Brussels and were asked what took them so long they confessed to having been 'in a bit of a dust up.' It was a 'dust up' which earned Lt. Towers-Clarke the MC and Cpl. Timbrell the MM.

Meanwhile in Brussels itself champagne and tears flowed freely. The troops were inundated with gifts of flowers and wine. There was practically no opposition, the odd sniper or two being quickly dealt with. The contrast with the devastation of rural Normandy pervaded by the smell of death was overwhelming. The buildings were almost intact, the population sophisticated, the girls in particular being beautifully dressed. There was a gigantic depot with five thousand bottles of champagne and hundred of tons of food, intended for the supply of the German Officers' Messes throughout France, Belgium and Holland. Ernie remembers thousands of tins of button mushrooms and tinned meat of all kinds. The civilians tried to raid it but Anstruther-Gray kept them out saying 'Reservé pour le Militaire.' It was a night none of them ever forgot.

The Grenadier Guards pushed on straight through Brussels to Louvain, ten miles to the north, to where the Germans had retreated. The rest of them stayed on in the capital for two or three days. When they in turn moved on they left behind a French-speaking officer whose parents lived locally to prepare hotels for rest and recuperation centres for the war-weary troops, for whom the war began all over again in Louvain, the village where Lord Frederick Cambridge had met his death four years before.

The village of Heppen was being held by the 6th German Paratroop division which the Guards had been 'bumping into' all the way across France and Belgium. General Erdmann had been there the previous night urging his troops to fight to the bitter end and it was indeed a formidable struggle. Ernie accompanied Anstruther-Gray to the top of the church tower to assess the situation and they could see the German army mustering for a counter-attack. One of the leading tanks in Ernie's troop was commanded by one of his best friends, Sergeant Eric Moffat. As they prepared to attack Ernie urged him over the wireless to 'watch yourself Moff.' It was to no avail - his tank suffered a direct hit and he was killed instantly. The Marquis of Hartington, heir to the Duke of Devonshire and husband of JF Kennedy's sister, was killed in the same battle. He was running up the village street when a German officer ran out of a house and shot him at close range with a revolver. As he fell a civilian came out of a farmhouse and cradled him in her arms as he died. Ernie still has a letter from her.

Eventually after a bloody battle Heppen was taken, but again the regiment lost many of its best men and as the struggle went on and the troops began to lose heart the Commanding Officers and Squadron Commanders were called to a meeting by Major General Sir Brian Horrocks to be told that Montgomery had devised a plan to take Arnhem. The Guards Armoured Division were to charge through the 'crust' of the German army which was holding up the advance, enter Holland and drive straight on through Eindhoven and Nijmegen to Arnhem. There was only one road as the Germans had sabotaged the rest, and there was water on either side of that one road, so there was no room for manoeuvre. Between them and victory were seven bridges and in Horrocks' opinion it was like holding up seven needles and trying to thread them simultaneously with your eyes closed.

When he returned from the meeting Anstruther-Gray called the men together to relay the 'Little Man's' plan. The German army was, said Monty, in disarray, demoralised and beaten. Unfortunately in Ernie's opinion nobody had explained that to the Germans. The Guards were expected to execute this plan with battle-weary troops and worn-out tanks which had travelled at speed all the way from Normandy. They had recently lost many of their best men and knew at first hand what they were up against. But orders were to be obeyed. To encourage them they were told that squadrons of Typhoons would go ahead of them to clear the way.

By September 17th 1944 they had struggled as far as Eindhoven. The Dutch civilians were delirious with delight, rushing out to greet them waving huge red, white and blue flags. They were desperately hungry, but so glad to see them that they actually held up the advance. As far as they were concerned the war was over. Tragically it was far from the truth. As they watched, the 101st American Airborne and British 1st Airborne Divisions were dropping well in front of them and being picked off by machine-gun fire as they drifted down. Dakota pilots bringing them in had to fly through devastatingly heavy flak - it was in Ernie's opinion a miracle any of them survived. Unknown to the advancing troops the much feared 10th SS Division had been recuperating in Arnhem and were able to muster in its defence.

The Guards could do nothing to help, being ordered not to fire as they would merely massacre their own troops. They had to stand by and watch what Ernie describes as 'a bloody lash-up'. With paratroops dead before they reached the ground, Dakotas crashing and gliders on fire it was a scene of carnage. Eventually they pushed on to Grave Bridge where they found an SS man tied to every girder so that he didn't fall off when he fired the bazooka with which he was armed. The Grenadiers successfully attacked the bridge, after two Dutch Resistance fighters had bravely disconnected the plungers set to blow it up. It was afterwards known as 'Grenadiers Bridge.'

The next target was Nijmegen where the bridge was equally as big and strongly defended. Nijmegen itself was burning and Irish Guardsmen were lying dead all over the place. Ernie's eyes still fill with tears as he remembers the scene. He says that he had never yet read an account of that battle which gives sufficient credit to the part played by the Irish Guards as they yet again gave their all in an attempt to force the thread through one more eye of the needles. As predicted the single road presented them with continuing problems. If a tank was disabled the whole column came to a halt while the bulldozers were called up to push it off the road and into the water. They were finally brought to a halt at Elst by a one-armed German Major with an 88mm gun.

They pulled in and took the opportunity to distribute rations and mail which had finally caught up with them. There were two more Beverley lads in Ernie's troop - both sadly killed later in the war. One of them opened a letter from home and whooped with laughter. "Listen to this," he crowed. "We've got a hero in our midst." His mother had sent him a cutting from the Beverley Guardian in which there was a vivid description of how Sergeant George Ernest Teal had burst into Brussels and armed only with a rifle had gone from house to house shooting the occupying Germans and virtually liberating the city single-handed! Poor Ernie wished the ground would open up and swallow him.

It eventually emerged that what had happened was that an enthusiastic reporter had been talking to Ernie's Mum, who had told him of her son's letter describing the re-taking of Brussels and the hand-to-hand fighting, bayoneting SS men in the streets. Always one to make a good story better, he obviously inherited his talents from his mother and by the time she and the reporter had added their mites the truth had become somewhat distorted and the 48,000 troops with Ernie had somehow been overlooked.

It was also at Elst, known as 'The Island', that Ernie yet again narrowly escaped death. He was at that time in command of a tank and had been told to maintain his position. Shells were exploding in front and behind them and in the driver's opinion they were trying to drop one straight down the turret and they should take evasive action. Despite Ernie's protests he put the tank into reverse and almost immediately two shells dropped exactly where they had been. As they withdrew Anstruther-Gray brought a wounded man to them - he had had his bottom jaw shot away. They also collected the Commander of another knocked out tank, a Corporal Catling, plus eight or nine prisoners, who all rode on the back of the tank. As they started to pull back a 'Moaning Minnie' trench mortar dropped behind them and blew off their 'passengers.' Ironically the only fatality was Corporal Catling - all the Germans were uninjured.

The tanks were sitting ducks as they moved in single file along the raised road and the enemy gun-emplacements were so well camouflaged that the Typhoons couldn't spot them from the air. Eventually, despite the pleas of the paratroopers to 'hurry up for God's sake' they were forced to pull back to Nijmegen. It was there that another of those coincidences with which Ernie's life was littered was to set the scene for 'the soldier's return.'

# Chapter 9

## THE SOLDIERS RETURN

The withdrawal to Nijmegen necessitated the finding of billets. Temporarily halted, the troops had to be provided with accommodation and as always the tanks merely pulled up in the street and the houses were requisitioned wholesale. Ernie walked into the house assigned to him and saw a woman at the sink washing the dishes. In typical fashion he dispensed with introductions, picked up a cloth and said, "Hello. I'll dry up for you!" The woman was, naturally, astonished. They were, he surmised, a Jewish family as they were called Abrahamson - mother Cora, father and a little girl called Angee - and Ernie stayed with them until October.

Nijmegen was shelled nightly and in addition German snipers hidden in the sewers emerged under cover of darkness to shoot unwary allied soldiers. Ernie was lodged in the attic, kept awake by the shells whistling overhead as the Germans tried desperately to retake Nijmegan Bridge. Mr. Abrahamson was an architect and the house was beautiful. Angee was just a few months old and pitifullly undernourished. Ernie immediately wrote to Doris telling her of the baby's plight and she sent parcels of orange-juice, cod-liver oil and dried milk. A firm friendship was forged, and Ernie vowed that one day he would take Doris to meet them.

While they were 'resting' in Nijmegen there was a brief hilarious interlude concerning a pig. A Lt. Jardine, in civilian life a wealthy land-owner and relative of the famous cricketer, celebrated his 21st birthday. Michael Hamilton, related to the Duke of Hamilton, decided the occasion should be marked in some style, and asked Ernie, renowned for his resourcefulness, if he could acquire a pig! Ernie, of course knew where there were some but said he would require the use of a Scout Car and two 'helpers', Guardsman Ted Olive and Sergeant Robinson. The pigs were on a farm in no-man's-land, near to where the Hampshire Regiment were dug in, who advised them against venturing in as the Germans regularly visited the farm to replenish their own supplies and would no doubt be keeping watch. Naturally Ernie ignored them and had soon killed two pigs with the aid of his captured German Mauser rifle. Then a fine specimen ran out between him and the Scout Car where an already nervous Sgt. Robinson had stayed on watch. Ernie dropped to his knees, took aim and fired. The bullet went straight through the pig and narrowly missed Sgt. Robinson. The three pigs were hastily loaded into the car and they fled back to Nijmegan. Michael Hamilton duly organised his pig roast and the other two victims were jointed by a butcher-friend of Cora Abrahamson's and shared out amongst Ernie's troop and their Dutch hosts.

After the long German occupation there were inevitably recriminations amongst the Dutch population. The British troops had been warned not to interfere in local disputes, but it was often difficult. A neighbour of the Abrahamsons had a sixteen-year-old daughter who had fallen in love with a German soldier. Once the Germans moved out she was accused of collaboration, the penalty for which was head-shaving, tarring and feathering. Cora begged Ernie to intervene, which he did, but it was pointed out to him that he wouldn't always be there to protect her. The soldiers were also badgered for grenades, which would be lobbed through the windows of suspected collaborators.

Ernie made other friends during his month's stay in the Dutch town. While out walking he met a party of nuns gathering fire-wood and as always offered his help. After that he met them quite often, taking a particular fancy to a young novice called Sister Regina. One day she wasn't with the others and when he enquired why was told that she was in trouble for talking and joking with him. This troubled Ernie and he presented himself at the convent and asked to see the Mother Superior, Mother Benedicta, who told him that he must not talk to Sister Regina as he did as it unsettled her. On one occasion Ernie had asked her if she had to shave off her hair and in reply she had pulled off her wimple and veil and allowed her hair to cascade down to her waist. This had been reported to Mother Benedicta, who was mightily displeased. Ernie, forthright as ever, expressed the opinion that it was a shame such a bonny lass would never marry and was told in return that she was already married - to God.

Despite these differences Ernie remained friends with the nuns and frequently visited the convent. One day he inadvertently came upon a room full of wounded German troops, but when he expressed his disapproval was told that to the nuns they were all 'people' and that during the German occupation they had hidden and tended the Allied soldiers. Although unconvinced Ernie didn't give them away.

In October the Coldstreams were once more on the move, through Sittard and at last over the border into Germany. For the first time they were on 'the sacred soil of the Fatherland.' As they moved through the towns and villages the civilians were chased out and fled into Holland. The smell of victory was in the nostrils of the Allied forces and sometimes went to their heads. A huge pig wandering along the side of the road was thought to resemble Herman Goering and summarily shot. The German civilians were robbed of all their possessions and a dim view taken of any resistance.

A village called Hillensberg which they took over reminded Ernie of a pre-war English village - little farmhouses with pigs, chickens and geese. At one house they encounted a prosperous-looking parson, very well-fed and volubly pro-British. He said he had had nothing to do with the fighting and had no sympathy for the Nazis. Despite this Anstruther-Gray ordered a search of his large house which revealed a book of photographs illustrating the bombing of Coventry, many letters glorifying the German invasion of Europe and a profusion of Swastikas. In the cellar were sacks and sacks full of money which were promptly confiscated!

One of Ernie's prize possessions throughout the war was his 'hooky' - a loo-stick with a sharpened sickle on the end, with which he used to dispatch unwary chickens. It was now employed to dispatch the parson's flock of geese, which were quickly plucked and eaten with great relish. Ernie still has some of the letters taken from the house, which he kept as momentoes.

Life in the village during that October and November was good. There were trees full of ripe fruit, plenty of chickens, warm fires and a break from fighting. After the hell of Holland it was a most welcome relief. December came and with it the snow and rumours of a German surrender. Every night the sky to the south was lit up with gun-fire. That, they said, was Patton attacking the Siegfreid Line. In reality it was Field Marshal Rundstedt advancing on them in the Ardennes offensive. The Guards were dispatched to Belgium to form a barrier between the Germans and Antwerp. After so much optimism it was a disheartening set-back.

The tanks set off in blinding snow. Ernie's Sherman soon broke down and they got left behind. They eventually got it re-started and drove out of Germany through Holland and into Belgium but they still hadn't caught up. They had clocked up a huge mileage in appalling conditions and decided to halt for the night. They pulled into the forecourt of a big house through a pair of 'very fancy gates'. The owner turned out to be an extremely pro-German Belgian who tried to deny them access, warning them that 'Adolf will soon get you'. He was persuaded otherwise with the help of a threatening sten-gun and reluctantly showed them into an unfurnished room. By now thoroughly fed up Ernie and his mates turned him and his wife out of their bedroom and used their beds. As they left next morning they unfortunately ran into his fancy gates! "At least", said Ernie, "he'll remember we've been here."

The Ardennes Offensive was Germany's last major effort of the war. Ernie and his crew eventually caught up with their division in Belgium and rejoined the convoy but the appalling conditions had played havoc with discipline and tanks were scattered all over the area. It was still snowing and blowing and as a girl rode past them on a bicycle her dress blew up 'showing all she'd got'. They were travelling at 20mph - the Sherman's maximum speed - and the distraction was disastrous. Even as Ernie's driver turned his head to say 'Look at that Duke' the tank ahead braked suddenly. He made a valiant attempt to avoid it but in swerving he caught the tracks of the front tank and slewed right across the road. A collision between two thirty-two ton tanks makes quite a noise and the dozing crews had a rude awakening. In addition the road was completely blocked bringing the hundred or so tanks behind them to a halt. Some tried to pull round the obstruction but the mines had only been cleared on the main highway and several were blown up. Eventually the disabled tank was bulldozed into the dyke and the convoy once more pushed on through the snow.

The Guards Armoured Division regrouped in Neer Heylissem where the civilians greeted them with enthusiasm. Hubert Moyens, proprietor of the local paint business, took Ernie home to meet his wife, daughter and son. Ernie couldn't believe his luck. There was a white-hot stove and they brewed him acorn coffee and shared their meagre rations with him. The tank had been 'parked' in the middle of the street but when Hubert asked 'what about the tank?' Ernie, warm for the first time in days, told him it could take care of itself.

The battalion remained in Neer Heylissem over Christmas. The men had a celebration dinner in the school while the officers were entertained in a country house just outside the town. On Christmas Eve they had all been given bottles of spirits. Ernie as a Sergeant received brandy, whisky and gin, all 'liberated' from the Brussels Depot. Already fairly happy one night he met a local man who offered to show him his pigeons, a lifelong passion of Ernie's, making the invitation irresistible. His new friend took him to his dark little house and introduced him to his wife and numerous children. Ernie produced a bottle and they began a convivial evening. He remembers little else of that night. Somebody found him lying in the snow and carried him back to Hubert Moyens' house. Unused to strong drink of any kind the mixture of brandy and whisky proved to be lethal. When he did wake up he thought he was dying.

At 3.30am the bedroom door was flung open and an officer dressed in a fur-collared flying coat and flying boots ordered them to 'get up - the Germans are here'.

Ernie didn't move. 'What's wrong with him?' he demanded, and was told he was drunk. 'Well sober him up and get him outside,' they were told. Somebody dressed him with difficulty in his flying suit and they dropped him unceremoniously through the turret of his tank. They set off in the still blinding snow with no real idea of where they were and ploughed on up and down through the drifts and the dykes. As the atmosphere inside the tank became more and more unbearable they were forced to stop. Ernie was lifted out and between bouts of sickness managed to utter the immortal words 'Je suis malade'. A woman and a young girl took him inside their house and gave him black coffee. He told them it was the garlic in the food he had been given the night before which had upset him!

Failing to find the Germans they returned to Neer Heylissem where they were treated like conquering heroes. They discovered later that the Americans had stopped the enemy before the British had got anywhere near them. They stayed in the village until January and Ernie still corresponds with his hosts, the hospitable Moyens.

In January rumours began to circulate that they were to cross the Rhine. There were a few local skirmishes, then convoys carrying boats began to pass through Neer Heylissem. The 'big offensive' was about to be launched.

In March 1945 the Guards Armoured Division approached the Rhine. Ernie accompanied Anstruther-Gray to have a look at the river itself. Through binoculars as far as they could see all the bridges were down. At the time they didn't know that in fact there was one remaining bridge intact in the American sector at Remagen. Montgomery had promised that within twenty-four hours he would throw eight Bailey bridges across the Rhine and the offensive would be spearheaded by the 51st Highland Division. First though the enemy positions were to be hit by the 'biggest barrage ever' carried out by every gun in the Second Army and every plane the Airforce could put in the air.

The Lancasters and Halifaxes passed over in daylight and Ernie estimates that there must have been a thousand or more. This was followed by a forty-eight hour non-stop barrage . To try to shut out the appalling noise they dug holes in the ground under their parked tanks and crawled into them to sleep. Or at least to try to sleep.

The ground was shaken continuously 'as though a giant was stirring the earth like a pudding' as Ernie puts it. Twigs and branches were shaken from trees. When it finally stopped British and American paratroops were dropped and the 51st Highlanders began their assault. But the Germans had been well dug-in, close to the river, and in their anxiety to avoid their own troops much of the bombardment had passed over the enemy positions. They were waiting for the allies and soon rafts of dead bodies were floating down the river. Ernie and company could only watch helplessly as the gallant 51st fought to the death.

Undaunted the 15th Scottish Division followed their comrades, then the Engineers went in to build bridges. What they didn't know was that the Americans had already crossed at Remagen further to the south and gradually resistance began to crumble but once across the river they were held up yet again at Goch and Wesel. There they found a terrible mess. German troops had been hung from trees or shot by the SS as they tried to retreat. In one house they found an old woman and three German soldiers sitting round a table where they had been playing cards. They were all dead but without a mark on them, killed by the blast from the exploding shells.

*The Abrahamsons.*

*Text on reverse says:
"Dear Mrs. Teal,
Holland writing again, this is a
photograph of our wedding.
Please will you send us one of
your wedding. We would like one.
We try to learn your husband
speaking Dutch, but up to now
he's only speaking Double Dutch.
Yours sincerely".*

*Lt. Freiherr Von der Heyden,
Commanding Officer of the
6th German Parachute
Regiment.*

*December 23rd, 1944, the Ardennes offensive.*
*Hubert Moyens and family with Ernie.*

*The Moyens*
*on a visit*
*to Walkington.*

77

At last they were on the move again. This time it was foot down and head for Bremen. The familiar names flashed up on the maps - Hamburg, Wilhelmshaven - all these years of fighting and at last the end was in sight. Surely this time it was for real. In one village they passed through they found a deserted egg-packing factory and loaded trays of them into the tank, but before they could eat them all the bottom ones went bad with the heat from the engine. In another village they found sacks of sugar - a very welcome supplemet to their diet. Then they approached the village of Burg which in Ernie's opinion would have won a 'Britain in Bloom' competition hands down.

As they progressed across Germany the routine was for a German-speaking officer to telephone ahead to the next village and to ask to speak to the Burgomaster. He would tell him that if he surrendered there would be no killing or looting and no burning. If there was resistance they would have no hesitation in using their flame-throwers to raze the village to the ground. The Burgomaster of Burg assured them that the Germans had left and that there would be no resistance. Unfortunately at the time an SS officer was holding a Luger to his head.

The tanks rolled into the village, the crews relaxed and unsuspecting. When the narrow main street was filled the 6th German Parachute Regiment struck. They disabled the first and last tanks then systematically destroyed the rest. The remaining tanks pulled back and the Commanding Officer in a fury ordered that the village be burnt to the ground. Ernie remembers with horror seeing a young blonde girl running down the street clutching a baby to her breast and thinking that that was just what Doris and baby Christine would be like.

As they advanced once more into the now devastated village it was a complete shambles. Anstruther-Gray shouted at them to slow down as they were over-running their own dead and wounded. One soldier cracked under the strain and started firing his Bren-gun at random killing his compatriots as well as the enemy until he in his turn was shot. Ernie was ordered to back his tank into a hedge and camouflage it to ambush the Germans as they withdrew. Jack Carron, Ernie's erstwhile poaching partner and 'a complete nutter' had a Scout Car with twin Brownings mounted on the front and twin Spandaus on the back. Enraged by the loss of so many of his companions he opened fire on a truck-load of German soldiers, setting it on fire, then started shooting them as they tried to escape until his Commanding Officer arrived and put him under immediate arrest.

After all the horrors of the previous five years this experience was probably the worst Ernie and his troop suffered, made more so by the fact that it was nearly all over. Asked how he felt then he says you didn't have to think about what you were doing, just do it. 'Ours not to reason why . . . . ' Death was always there, always just around the next corner, and you were always frightened. Although this is one place he hasn't revisited his daughter and son-in-law have and have told him it's all been rebuilt as though nothing had ever happened there.

One rule Ernie found it very difficult to comply with was the 'non-fraternisation' edict, with Anstruther-Gray threatening to shoot anyone who disobeyed. Ernie found it impossible to hate the ordinary folk who had willy-nilly been caught up in this war and used to surreptitiously give cigarettes to the prisoners and try to help the wounded, but some of the soldiers had become embittered and brutalised by the prolonged fighting and atrocities were committed by both sides. It was also sometimes difficult to make excuses for the 'children' of the Hitler Youth who were fully armed and had been brain-washed into fanaticism.

As they advanced across Germany they had come across Prisoner of War camps and it had given them great joy to release the allied prisoners especially if they were men from their own regiment who had been there since 1941. Many of these camps were very well run but the concentration camps were horrific beyond comprehension.

The final objective for the Guards Armoured Division was Cuxhaven on the Baltic coast where there was rumoured to be a V2 rocket base. The German civilians in the area were no longer patriotic, just frightened, and said Hitler was no good. They did however meet fierce opposition from the German Marines and the Navy. Montgomery had by now 'taken his foot off the accelerator' as he had wanted 'his' army to head for Berlin. Instead they were ordered to 'turn left for the Baltic'. On April 30th rumours circulated that the Fürher was dead and there was talk of peace. They were once more filled with hope. One of the tanks from Ernie's troop was dispatached to help the Engineers rebuild a bridge over a stream. The driver was Frank Lock from Beverley and their job was to give cover to the Sappers in case of opposition from the Volk Sturm, the German equivalent of our Home Guard. Suddenly there was an almighty explosion. The Volk Sturm had already struck by burying a sea-mine in the road. Designed to destroy a ship it blew the tank and its crew to pieces. The only recognisable thing that remained was the gun. Ernie was once again devastated. Frank had been with him throughout the war.

Cuxhaven was still occupied by thousands of German soldiers, all sullen, all still armed. With them were thousands more civilians, wary and watchful, lining the roads. The British troops were ordered to keep all their guns loaded and at the ready. Ernie was filled with foreboding. They had a long column of tanks but if it came to a fight they would be hopelessly outnumbered. As they entered the port they came under fire from a destroyer anchored out in the bay. A few tanks were damaged but the shelling soon stopped. The Naval Base was filled with destroyers and submarines and the airfield with planes.

They were told that the 6th German Parachute Regiment was ready to surrender but before they did Sergeant Teal was told by his Commanding Officer, Colonel Gooch, that he 'had a little job for him'. He was to take two Corporals and escort a German Colonel - the Garrison Commander of Cuxhaven - in a Staff Car to battalion headquarters to receive the surrender. The Colonel, now an elderly man, handed over his Luger to Ernie telling him that it had never fired a shot. The German driver was only young and had in fact lived in London for several years before the war.

When they arrived at the Garrison Ernie was understandably nervous. Apart from anything else they were all bigger than him! However at a barked command from the Colonel they neatly stacked their arms in the centre of the parade ground and stood to attention. There was some head shaking and muttering but a shouted command from the Colonel soon quelled it and they subsided. It was, says Ernie, a chilling moment.

Two or three days later the 6th Paratroopers as promised came marching into town, colours flying, boots polished and officers resplendent in full dress uniform complete with swords. They presented arms and formally surrendered. They were followed by tanks, armoured cars and trucks. The Guards constructed a huge barbed-wire enclosure in which to confine them with a Sherman tank on watch every ten yards around the perimeter, but by now discipline was relaxed and they turned a blind eye to the arrival of German wives and the absconding of the German soldiers.

Sir William Anstruther-Gray came to talk to the Coldstreamers. He had been with them throughout the whole war. He patted the guns and said the last shot had been fired in anger. The next day the surrender would be signed and within the hour he would be gone, flying back to his constituency. He predicted that there would be an early General election and that the Socialists would win. He gave them each the equivalent of twenty-five pounds in German marks and wished them all well.

Ernie was glad the war was virtually over but sad that his Commanding Officer was leaving them.

On May 8th the surrender was signed. There was Victory in Europe.

*"Gibraltar holiday".*

*All Hallows Church, Walkington, in 1987.*

*The interior of All Hallows Church for Julie's wedding.*

*The 1988 Hayride. Bob Champion, with Mrs. Edith Waterworth, senior.*

*Ernie at the 1990 Hayride.*

*Right:*
*Doris and Ernie,*
*"singing along".*

*Below:*
*1990 Hayride, assembling*
*in the stackyard.*

*Left to right: Pat, Ernie, Doris and Christine at the Palace.*

*Doris and Ernie on New Year's Eve, 1989, after announcing
Ernie's honour to the entire family.*

*Right:*
*Guardsman Busby at*
*Ernie's "This Is Your Life".*

*Left:*
*Ernie with his*
*Investiture photograph.*

*Golden Wedding Celebrations.*
*Left to right: Daughter Christine Elston, Doris, John Elston, Ernie, Mike*
*Rhodes, daughter Pat Rhodes.*

*Floral tributes and cards!*

*George Ernest Teal, MBE.*
*Photo courtesy of Anthony David Baynes, Riverside Studio, Hull.*

# Chapter 10

## THE AFTERMATH

For Ernie the war as such ended in Cuxhaven and he reverted to being a peacetime soldier. The end of his original four years was of course long past but he was still committed as a reservist and it was some time before he was demobbed. He missed his Commanding Officer, Major Sir William Anstruther-Gray who reverted to being a Member of Parliament. He eventually succeeded his father, Lord Kilkenny, and took his seat in the House of Lords where he died after a heart attack, watched on television with dismay by Ernie.

A few days after VE Day the Guards Armoured Division was ordered to hand over its tanks in Hamburg. They would once more become infantry. It was all to be done properly. They drove from Cuxhaven to Hamburg where the tanks were driven away over the crest of a hill to be loaded onto ships. The Guards came marching after them and Montgomery took the salute then made a speech in which he said the war wasn't quite over yet. There was still Japan. He confidently predicted that the Allies would win but it would probably cost a million more lives as the Japs would fight to the death. Regular soldiers would be dispatched to the Japanese front forthwith.

Although used to destruction on a massive scale Ernie was nevertheless appalled when he saw Hamburg. Ships had been quite literally blown out of the water, the debris landing up to a mile and a half inland. The Guards didn't stay there long. Out of the *original* battalion of twelve hundred and fifty there were less than a hundred left and they were loaded into trucks heading for Bad Godesburg. As they drove through Cologne no-one spoke. The victim of the thousand bomber raid it had been almost completely flattened with hardly any buildings left standing and with just 'bits of roads' through the rubble. The stench of death was everywhere.

Bad Godesburg was a spa town and the Guards were lodged in the former SS barracks. This was indeed luxury - proper toilets and a squad of German civilians to look after them. The 'looking after' became mutual and Ernie's natural talent for bartering was allowed full rein. The currency was cigarettes and coffee with which you could 'buy' anything, including the favours of the lady of your choice. In fact demobbed German soldiers sent their wives out 'on the streets' in order to obtain supplies of cigarettes.

Ernie as usual got on well with the locals, fraternisation no longer being forbidden. He was - and is - a great believer in the fact that if you get to know people you won't want to fight against them. One elderly lady in particular he befriended was Frau Zuttermeister, a widow in her seventies. She had lost two sons in Russia and her husband had been killed in one of the last air-raids of the war. He had been chopping firewood when the siren went and although he sent his wife to the shelter he didn't bother going himself. When she emerged she found he had been killed by the blast from a bomb dropped by a US Airforce Flying Fortress. Despite this she wasn't bitter and welcomed Ernie into her home where he often stayed for the weekend.

He had originally started talking to her in the street and had given her some coffee.

She owned a little house with an orchard filled with apple trees and Ernie loved it and her. It was almost like being back at home with his Mum. As November approached he was told that he was forbidden to go into one of the rooms of the house and on his birthday, November 1st 1945, he found out why as she revealed a beautiful birthday cake made from ingredients carefully hoarded from her meagre rations and iced with his name and 'Happy Birthday'. He was very touched. Sadly after the war he lost touch with her as he did with another friend he made, Frau Magda Lutz.

When Hitler visited Godesburg he used to stay at the Hotel Kaiserhof and Ernie put his barter system into operation with the owner, 'a big fat fellow', and his wife. The man was scared of Ernie as he had been a top man in the town during the Nazi regime. He still lived in a big house filled with beautiful paintings but these didn't interest Ernie. He swapped his coffee and cigarettes for sheets and pillowcases from the hotel, naturally of the finest quality and which lasted the young Teal family for years.

Duties in Godesburg were quite light. They had to maintain a watch on the civilian population, which included regular delousing sessions, and try to prevent the revival of overt patriotism. This last exercise was not entirely successful as despite a curfew there would be fresh flowers on the War Memorial every morning.

During this time Montgomery announced that all soldiers who had served throughout the entire way would be sent on a month's leave to Austria. In parties of twenty they travelled by truck across Germany following the Rhine through Munich and into Austria to Pertisau on Lake Achensee. It was a beautiful place, surrounded by mountains topped with snow. They were housed in a big 'posh' hotel used by high-ranking Nazis during the war as a safe refuge for their wives. A group of coloured American soldiers had been there before the British and they hadn't been well behaved so the local population were wary of the newcomers. Ernie and his friends rowed across the lake to a village on the opposite bank and the adults fled in terror but the children were braver and stayed to talk. Ernie gave them sweets and cigarettes for their parents and took lots of photographs with his looted Leica camera.

The village was quite primitive, a farming community composed of wooden chalets which the inhabitants shared with their cattle for mutual warmth. Ernie would buy things from the shops in Pertisau to take to them as he was appalled by their poverty. By contrast to this rural peace the infamous Mauthausen concentration camp - the Death Camp - was only a short distance away and there was a huge tunnel near Pertisau where aircraft had been built, all reminders of the recent conflict. Despite this Ernie fell totally in love with the place and vowed that one day he would return, with Doris.

When he arrived back in Godesburg he found that Number 26 Group - his - was due for demobilisation in January 1946. There was a lot of interchanging between units as the armies made ready for withdrawal. Ernie spent a week with an American battalion, mostly coloured lads, who were having the time of their lives with the local 'ladies of the town'. A plentiful supply of nylon stockings ensured their gratification. There was also a thriving black market with gold Hunter watches and cameras freely available, many of them looted from Russia.

Ernie's erstwhile Commanding Officer, Colonel Dickie Gooch, was by now a Brigadier and he came to inspect the men and talk to them before they returned to England. He asked Ernie what he was going to do and when he said he fancied being a male nurse in a mental hospital he said he didn't think it was Ernie's cup of tea. He suggested he should stay on in the army and go with him to 'fight the Commies in Malaya', promising to put a crown above his stripes. But Ernie was not to be bribed. He just wanted to get home to Doris and Christine.

The day before demob the battalion was paraded on the square in front of Colonel Roddy Hill and a 'real b . . . . of an RSM'. As Number 26 Group stood on the parade ground all NCO's - not Guardsmen - were told to fall out and form up on the right. There were thirty of them. "Right," said the RSM. "I'll teach them how to say goodbye to their regiment. I'll kill the b . . . . . . s." They were marched round and round the square until they were exhausted. Even Ernie, strict disciplinarian that he was, was moved to shout out "You b . . . . . . s." What a thing to remember his last day by.

Next morning his fellow Guardsmen came to say farewell, then they climbed into a truck and headed for the Railway Station and a train for Calais. Ernie was loaded up with loot including two telescopic rifles. Orders had been issued that anyone found smuggling arms into England would have his demobilisation cancelled and would serve up to twenty years with hard labour. Ernie panicked, dismantled the rifles, stowed them under a mattress and abandoned them. He did however keep a clockwork revolving musical Christmas tree holder which still revolves and plays every year in his Walkington home and has become a family heirloom.

Ernie was appalled by the behaviour of the troops as the train travelled through the French countryside. Youngsters lined the sides of the railway tracks begging for food and soldiers would hurl abuse as well as tins of meat at them and they also, in Ernie's view, treated the French girls in a totally callous fashion.

At Calais Ernie boarded a ship for Dover then took a train to London where he was issued with a navy suit with white chalk stripes. He was, after nearly nine years, back in civvy street.

Some twenty-five years later Ernie was looking at a holiday catalogue when the name 'Pertisau' leapt out of the page at him. There was a coach tour to the very place where he had spent that magical month in 1945. He immediately booked places for himself and Doris. They travelled along the familiar route, following the Rhine, through Munich and into Russia. As the coach turned a corner he shouted, "There it is!" Doris thought it looked like fairyland.

They were staying in the Hotel Reiser, whose proprietress was Frau Reiser. Ernie had taken his wartime photographs with him, and showed them to her. One of them was of herself and he was able to tell her that her mother had been tossed by a cow and broken her arm. They visited another hotel where a woman was tending a rose-bed. He told her he had stayed there in 1945 and she said she had lived there then and invited them in for coffee.

When they visited the village on the other side of the lake there was only one building left of those he had photographed. A man walked by somewhat the worse for drink, but Ernie nevertheless produced his photographs and repeated his story of being there in 1945. He took them to a restaurant opposite where they were invited in for coffee, and again much interest was shown in the photographs.

Several excursions were included in the package holiday and on one of these the coach driver was an Austrian, the courier a Dutchman who spoke both English and German. He told the driver there was a man on the coach who had been in the area

91

*A German family Ernie made*
*friends with*
*in Bad Godesburg.*

*The birthday cake!*
*Inscription on back: George's birthday cake, with love from Mother".*

# LETTER No. 2

### BY THE

# COMMANDER-IN-CHIEF

### ON

# NON-FRATERNISATION

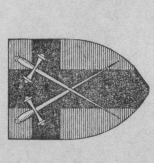

## TO ALL MEMBERS
## OF 21 ARMY GROUP

1. I have been considering the present orders about non-fraternisation.

We cannot let-up on this policy.

2. But these orders need no longer apply to small children.

3. Members of the British Forces in Germany will be allowed to speak to, and play with, little children. This will come into effect at once. In all other respects the orders issued by me in the card dated March 1945 will remain in force.

B. L. Montgomery

Field Marshal,
C-in-C, 21 Army Group.

12 June 1945

*Orders on non-fraternisation!*

93

*'With love from Irmgard,
Anita, Hanneliese!'.
Three of Ernie's friends
in Bad Godesburg, 1945.*

*"A lasting memory of Hanneliese
or John-Elizabeth, your little
German girlfriend. A remembrance
of beautiful friendship and happy
days in Bad Godesburg, Germany".*

*Irma as a little girl in Pertisau in 1945.*

*Irma, husband and parents, taken when Ernie and Doris*
*re-visited Pertisau in 1985.*

in 1945, and once more Ernie produced his photographs. The driver recognised one of the children, who by a wonderful coincidence was the cook at the hotel where the coach was stopping for Apple Strudel.

When they arrived at the hotel he was taken into the bakehouse to meet the 'little girl', now a large Frau! She was able to identify several of the other children and directed Ernie to yet another hotel where he went with Doris, the courier and the driver, who shouted, "Hello Frau Irma Reisch. There's an English friend of yours to see you." Although she protested she had no English friends she came and looked at the photographs and was able to identify not only herself but her sister. There was great excitement and her father and her husband came to join them. Her father got his photographs out and they were all set for a long session of 'story-swapping and Schnaps-supping.'

He had been a prisoner-of-war in Russia for ten years, and when he was freed no transport was provided to get him home, so he set out to walk. After a few miles he was stopped by a Russian peasant who stole his boots. He stumbled on bare-foot only to be stopped again by another Russian who this time gave him some boots. Many of the Russians in fact did help him and he made his way across Russia to Yugoslavia where he was not treated so well. When he eventually arrived home it was to find that his wife, believing him dead, had gone off with another man. However he did qualify for three pensions - from the German and Austrian armies and his old-age pension.

Ernie and Doris were having the time of their lives in Pertisau. They photo-graphed everything and everybody but when they took the films into a shop to have them developed to their intense disappointment they hadn't come out, there was a fault with the camera. That evening in the bar Ernie was telling the barman in German all about it when a young woman who had been sitting further along the bar interrupted. She had overheard his tale of woe and was intrigued by it. She had worked as an au-pair in London and spoke good English. She fetched her husband and introduced him. He was the Managing Director of the Mercedes Benz organi-sation in Stuttgart, and was, says Ernie, 'a wonderful fellow.'

Next day he and his wife took Doris and Ernie back to all the places they'd visited and re-took all the photographs with their own camera. They also took them across the border into Bavaria to Tegernsee where Ernst Rohmn and his brownshirts had been butchered by the SS. They visited an enormous beer-cellar which held upwards of a thousand people and where they were served with white sausage, bread and huge steins of beer. Ernie, mindful of the travelling to come, asked for 'just a small one' but was told they didn't serve babies!

By the time Ernie and Doris rejoined the party at the hotel the coach had left for Italy on another expedition. It was to return the next day to pick them up and take them home. It was almost new, a one million mark German built Mercedes, but after being driven non-stop by its team of three Belgian drivers it arrived back 'knackered' according to Ernie and leaking oil. Their courier said he had tried to make them stop but they insisted they didn't speak either English, French or German! Ernie's Managing Director friend was furious and said they had ruined the vehicle.

In the meantime Ernie and Doris and the rest of the fifty-strong party were stranded. Frau Reiser understandably wanted some guarantee of reimbursement before she would accommodate them for an extra night as most of them had spent up. She did agree however to let them sleep in the lounges on settees and armchairs. To Ernie and Doris's acute embarrassment their new-found German friends booked them a room and despite their protestations insisted they used it, so they at least spent the final night of their memorable holiday in comfort.

# Chapter 11

## JACK OF ALL TRADES

Doris travelled down from Beverley to London to meet Ernie when he was demobbed, leaving baby Christine with her in-laws, then together they boarded the train back north. At last they were going home.

Home was in fact to be the medieval house in Highgate where Ernie had been brought up. His parents had moved round the corner to the Old Friary in Friars Lane off Eastgate, occupying the same site as Armstrongs' car component factory where Doris had worked on munitions during the war. It belonged to the Minster Old Fund, as did the Highgate house and was administered by a board of Trustees, amongst whom was 'Dodie' Whitehead, Ernie's old headmaster. It was he who suggested the Teals as tenants as he knew George Teal was 'handy with a trowel' and the Old Friary had a permanent problem with flooding which no-one seemed to be able to cure.

The building was originally the home of the Blackfriars, an order of Dominican monks dedicated to helping the community and with no connection with the Minster in whose shadow it stands. It was divided into three dwellings and the Teals rented one of these plus an orchard containing about eighty productive fruit trees and where they also kept pigs and chickens.

Although Ernie never lived there he did stay there once after his parents moved in in 1946. He confessed that he found it a creepy place, especially as it was lit by candles, one of which he took up to bed with him. He blew it out and got into bed but almost immediately heard a scraping and creaking from behind the ancient oak panelling. Then a voice said "There's only thee and me now lad," a phrase it repeated several times. Ernie leapt out of bed replying "Aye and as soon as I get my bloody trousers on there'll only be thee!" It was in fact his Dad trying to scare him - or maybe getting his own back for that long-ago lump of concrete.

Because the Blackfriars worked with the community they almost always built their Friaries in the centres of population and for this reason the buildings usually fall prey to modern development. It is very rare for them to survive intact and even rarer to be lived in by secular tenants. The first tenant after the Dissolution of the Monasteries in 1539 was Richard Fayrecliff. At that time the property included an orchard of one a half acres, the same orchard rented by Ernie's Mum and Dad more than four hundred years later. The soil surrounding the Friary was very fertile and grew wonderful plants.

In the nineteenth century Friars Lane was part of the main road into Beverley but when the level crossing over the railway was replaced by a pedestrian bridge it reverted to being a little rural enclave in the centre of the busy market town. People who lived there kept pigs, chickens, geese and horses and an old lady called Mrs Jude sold milk from her cottage. There was a communal pump for water and the little community was very close-knit.

In the eighteenth and early nineteenth centuries the Friary was owned by the Earls of Yarborough who in 1826 sold it to Richard Whiteing of Beverley Parks. A descendant of his with the same name owned part of the building until 1960. At some unknown date before 1861 it was divided into three separate houses and given the numbers 7, 9 and 11 Friars Lane. Margaret Whiteing lived in one part and in 1887 Canon Nolloth of Beverley Minster bought number 7 as a residence for his curate. In due course it became the property of the Minster and thus eventually home to the Teals.

The central 'house', number 9, has the longest record of occupation by one family, the Woodmanseys. Hilda, who became Mrs Lever, was born there in 1908 when it was the home of a washerwoman, Miss Annie Woodmansey. Mrs Lever's grandparents met at Burton Constable and moved to number 9 in the mid 1880's. Their young family included Annie who remained there until her final illness. She died in 1964, aged eighty-four.

Mrs Lever's parents, William Dunston and Ethel Woodmansey, Annie's sister, lived in Friars Lane in a two-bedroomed cottage but Ethel moved into the more spacious Friary with her parents for the birth of her children and eventually Hilda went to live there permanently, to be brought up by her grandparents and her Aunt Annie. She moved to Hull in 1926 when she was eighteen. Annie remained to care for her elderly parents. Her mother was blind and the family was poor but Annie numbered some of Beverley's best-known residents among her clientele. She spent long hours in the brick wash-house near the Friary garden gate, often washing by candle-light. She collected and delivered the laundry in a barrow. Otherwise she only left the house once a year to buy a pair of shoes in Evans' shop in the Market Place.

Annie also made wedding cakes to order, no mean feat in a house equipped with neither gas nor electricity. Landlord Mr. Whiteing refused to have either installed because of the amount of wood in the house. One would have thought the candles and oil lamps to be a much greater hazard.

Number 7, ultimately to become the home of Ernie's parents, was, in the early part of the century, occupied by Fred 'Grandad' Thomas who worked at Hodgson's Tannery and died in the 1930's. During the First World War he used to sit on the railway bridge and watch the Zeppelins! In the 1920's his daughter Florence and her husband Herbert Nicholson and their family shared his home but they eventually left after father and son-in-law quarrelled. His other daughter Gertie then moved in with her husband Jack Braithwaite and their family. It must have been crowded as half of this one third of the Friary was sub-let to the Ross family for seven shillings a week.

Number 7 the Friary was a wonderful place with a carved wooden cross at the top of the landing, carved fireplaces, wall paintings concealed by panelling and a 'confession chamber', a large cupboard entered through a door in the panelling where there was a fresco of a cross of thorns. No wallpaper or paint was allowed by the Minster Trustees however, and it was alive with mice, silverfish and the infamous 'blackclocks'. It also had more land than either numbers 9 or 11, Grandad Thomas paying a peppercorn rent for the orchard. Another condition of tenancy was that visitors must always be shown around on request.

When the Teals took over number 7 in January 1946 it was somewhat dilapidated and very damp. Its previous occupant had been a Mrs. Thompson who had taken in evacuees. It was also, as previously said, subject to flooding every time there was heavy rain. Ernie's father built a large concrete step in front of the property to direct the water round the side. Gas had by that time been laid on, but there was no electricity. He came to an agreement with the Trustees to pay for the cable being laid,

99

then they would fund the wiring of the house, but eventually they paid for it all. The only running water was from an outside tap and the toilet was also outside, but eventually a bathroom was installed, again by the Trustees.

The Teals remained in the house for twenty years, making many improvements and with a verbal agreement that it wouldn't be sold in their life time - an agreement that was to be broken when Armstrongs wanted to extend their factory, and they felt that all their efforts had been wasted. The first 'official' news they had of the sale was when the builder asked them to keep their chickens locked up as they were going to knock down the orchard wall!

Ironically Armstrongs' factory was only to be in use for less than twenty years more. It closed in 1981 and it was eventually demolished to make way for a high-class housing development adjacent to the Friary, now restored and in use as a Youth Hostel. When Ernie and Doris revisited it they couldn't recognise any of the rooms, the building now being opened out once more into a single unit. The only thing that was at all familiar was the pantry window!

By the time Doris and Ernie moved into number 6 Highgate it too had been refurbished, but it was still an old house, with all the inconveniences that implies including having no bathroom, but at least it was a house. They had very little money and Ernie refused to even consider living in London so the offer of the Highgate house for ten shillings a week was very welcome. Doris was by then pregnant with their second child and had originally been booked into a London hospital. By the time they moved to Beverley it was too late to book into a local hospital so Ernie's Aunt who lived in Cottingham invited her to stay there for the birth of their second daughter, Pat.

Ernie found it very hard to settle down to civilian life. He had gone off a carefree lad of eighteen and returned as a husband and the father of one - and almost two - children and a necessity to earn a living. For nearly ten years he had never had to think about paying bills or about where the next meal was coming from. Now he had to think of both, although Doris says he is still not interested in how much the bills are as long as they can pay them.

When he left the army he was entitled to four months pay as he had served for the entire war and he still had his reservist pay. He had signed on for four years 'with the colours' and eight on the reserve. Because of the war he had in fact stayed in the regular army for nine years so had three left as a reserve during which he would receive six pounds every three months. It wasn't much but it paid the rent.

Apart from his assertion to his CO that he was going to be a male nurse he hadn't really any idea what he wanted to do. His demob papers advised him to go to the labour exchange to ask about jobs in the area but when he presented his 'Part 2', his service record, which was excellent, he was told that records like that were ten a penny while jobs were almost non-existent. Ernie felt like hitting the man behind the counter but realised that there must be thousands in the same situation as himself.

While he was still on his four months paid leave an acquaintance called Roy Day asked hm to help him put up some commercial greenhouses in Long Lane to the south of the town. The extra money was more than welcome. Roy Day was really a woodman, hawking firewood around Beverley, but he had bought the land in Long Lane to grow lettuces and cucumbers. It meant that once the greenhouses were up Ernie was working mostly on his own, planting out seedlings and happy with his own company. Many prisoners of war were employed on the land at that time and at night as they stood by the roadside waiting for their transport back to their camp in what is now Bishop Burton College of Agriculture Ernie used to stop to chat with them. They were eager for news of their homeland where he had so recently been living.

When the planting out was finished he worked for a while in Kirby's woodyard in the town carrying timber about but it made his shoulders ache and he didn't stay very long. Doris remarks wryly that he didn't stay anywhere very long! Ernie with hindsight agrees that he was very unsettled, 'all twisted up' inside his head. Nowadays he says he would have received help to overcome the traumas of the war. In 1946 you just had to get on with life as best you could.

His next job was permanent 'nights' at Beverley laundry washing the bedding from Butlin's Holiday Camp at Filey. For that he earned six pounds a week - not a bad wage for those days. That again lasted for about a month then he told Doris he was going to join the Police, a step advocated by his father many years before as being a natural progression from the Guards. Doris was delighted. This at least seemed to offer longer term career prospects. Ernie says it lasted a month, Doris says it was three days - a week at the most.

In fact it was the Transport Police in Hull that had accepted Ernie's services on the strength of his rank of Sergeant in the Coldstream Guards. He very soon found however that it was a totally different way of life. His first assignment was to accompany the Duty Sergeant who was going to 'keep him right' to the docks to watch a railway luggage van being unloaded by dockers. He was told that 'they were all potential thieves' and he was to keep an eye on them.

He thought he had, but somehow a third of a huge cheese went missing, sliced neatly out of the whole. The Sergeant accused him of not watching but he swore he had never taken his eyes off them. Then sacks of sugar disappeared as well and the Sergeant said they would have to go to the gate and apprehend the culprits as they left. Although they never found the cheese they did recover some of the sugar. Ernie didn't like it. It was far too close to his own recent 'freelance' activities in Europe.

His next 'case' was one of illegal parking. A railway horse drawing a rully had been hitched to a lamp-post and had its feet on the pavement. That, said the Sergeant, was breaking the law and they would have him. He told Ernie to take the number of the cart while he went across the road to observe. As Ernie was laboriously writing it down in his notebook a big rough fellow came out of the house and asked him what he was doing. Ernie was still on probation and in civvies but he said he was Railway Police whereupon the driver said he had only called in briefly to light the oven to warm up his dinner while he stabled the horse. He was finding it difficult to cope as his wife had died the week before. Ernie was very sympathetic and sent him on his way. His Sergeant took a very different view. The man's wife, he said, was very much alive. The driver had been paying a call on his fancy woman!

Ernie's next mission was very different. A young couple travelling by train to their honeymoon destination had had their luggage stolen, including the bride's trousseau. Ernie was sent to a village between Hull and Goole to investigate. He and his Sergeant travelled by train and as they got off they saw a man crossing the line. He was quite clearly trespassing and Ernie, determined to redeem himself, set off after him shouting ferociously. The man fled with Ernie in hot pursuit. He eventually caught up with him in a field and rugby tackled him to the ground. The man protested

*This was the Friary garden where Armstrongs Factory later stood.*
*Eighty three trees were removed to make way for it.*

*Ernie's father and mother, George and Alice Teal, in the gardens of*
*the old Friary, August 1947.*

*Four generations.*
*Left to right: Ernie's mother, Alice, Granny Railton*
*with baby Christine, and Doris.*

*Ernie with his prize-winning onions in his Walkington garden, 1988.*

that he owned the land on either side of the track and was merely taking a short cut but Ernie had learned his lesson - he was no longer gullible. When his Sergeant arrived, somewhat out of breath, Ernie scornfully repeated the man's story, saying that his reason for running away was that Ernie's shouting had frightened him. His Sergeant however confirmed that the man was the owner of the farm. That was it. Ernie had had enough. He went to see the Chief and told him he wanted to quit. He would never, he said, be a conscientious policeman as he had far too much sympathy for the villains!

Doris was naturally upset when he came home with his tale of failure. Rationing restrictions were severe, they had two little girls and no money. Her mother wasn't over sympathetic saying she had made her bed and must lie on it. She would never have left Ernie but a brief respite with her own family would have been welcome. However better times *were* on the way. Ernie got a job at the Queensgate Quarry, the huge whitening works on the southern outskirts of the town, where he was to stay for the next eleven years.

He enjoyed his job there. It was in the open air, it was physical labour and nobody bothered him. It was a deep quarry where the chalk was broken up with a hammer and a pick. The four men in the team were paid a flat rate plus so much per ton. They each filled their own tubs which ran on rails down to the chalk face to be hauled back up when they were full. It suited Ernie. The harder he worked the more he could earn.

The winter of 1947 was the worst in living memory. It was hard getting enough chalk out to keep the mills supplied. Several gangs were employed to clear the snow so that the miners could get at the chalk. They were made up of men from the dole queues, often with inadequate clothes and shoes to protect them from the freezing weather. Even Ernie had permanent chilblains and suffered with 'hot-aches' in his hands. At weekends the German POW's helped out but rows used to frequently break out between them and the regulars.

The working day in the quarry was from 7.00am to 5.00pm six days a week with a half hour dinner break each day. The bad winter was followed by a lovely summer and the men were able to strip to the waist and all got very tanned. The foreman of the quarry was Jim Hood and he was in charge of blasting down the next chalk face for the men to work. Jack Hood worked with him. Once blasted down the railway lines were extended, the tubs taken in and the miners could break up the chalk and load it. The best quality chalk was used for whitening bread and in the ceramics and cosmetics industries. It was one of the biggest whitening works in the country.

On foggy days Herbert Jameson, the crane driver responsible for lowering the tubs down into the quarry and hauling them back up again, used to put a mark on the wire rope so that he would know when they they had reached the bottom. The miners would then detach the empty tub and fasten the rope to a full one and shout "Take it away Herbert".

It was quite a way down into the bottom of the quarry and for the men's convenience an earth toilet had been installed which hadn't been emptied for years. One foggy day the men loaded the container on top of a tub of chalk and shouted 'Take it away' as usual. As it crested the rise and tipped its evil smelling contents over the men at the top the foul language could be heard echoing and re-echoing around the walls of the quarry. Then the men at the bottom heard a rattling and realised that something was approaching down the rails at speed. It didn't sound like an empty tub, but only when it hit them did they find out it was a chemical toilet from the 'facilities' at the top of the site!

When Jim Hood left Ernie was 'promoted' to the shot-blasting team. The quarry was owned by Lawrence Foley-Judge who lived in North Cave, who was always urging the quarry manger, Frank Smith, to increase production. He said they should take the quarry twenty feet deeper where there was better quality chalk and, with a deeper face, a greater quantity as well, but he refused to let production be halted while they dug down and exposed the new face and blasted it off in stages. The only solution seemed to be to blow it all out at once, so Ernie and Jim Humphries with whom he was working drilled holes in the bottom of the quarry and inserted sticks of gelignite. When the chalk was blasted from the face of the quarry in the usual way it came forward and fell to the floor. Blown from below it went straight up in the air. The four men filling tubs had already been warned to take cover, but the exploding chalk went further than anyone - even Ernie - expected.

A chicken house belonging to Mick Wiffen from the garden of one of the four tied farm cottages near the quarry edge came flying down into the quarry with chickens flapping out of it in all directions. Half an hour later when the commotion had died down Herbert Jameson, the crane driver, shouted to Ernie that the manager, Frank Smith, wanted to see him. Ernie went into the office to find Frank sitting behind a table on which there was a huge lump of chalk which must have weighed a stone. It had landed at Black Mill, in the middle of Beverley Westwood, just missing Joyce Taylor who was out walking her dog. She was the sister of Ernie's long-time friend Bill Taylor and Ernie realised with horror that it might have killed her.

A hundred bullocks belonging to Billy Hannet had been grazing in a field at the back of the quarry. They stampeded and ran through the grounds of Beverley Grammar School and into the town. Frank asked Ernie what he'd been thinking of to cause such havoc. Ernie said defensively that he'd been told to blow it out. How was he to know that it would 'rain all over the plot.' At least production wasn't held up!

It was in 1949 while Ernie was working in the quarry that Walt Sissons, a workmate, told him he had moved into a new council house on the first council estate to be built in the village of Walkington some three miles west of Beverley. However, he didn't like it. The rent at eighteen shillings a week was more than he could afford, and he would rather live in Beverley. By now Ernie who was superbly fit was earning eight pounds fifteen shillings a week with bonuses and over-time and longed to live in the country, and without consulting Doris said, "We'll swap!" He just went home and said, "We're moving." He went to see Teddy Kell, Clerk to the Minster Trust, his Highgate landlord, who agreed in principle as he was anxious to do all he could for ex-servicemen. Then Ernie asked the advice of Herbert Jameson the crane-driver who lived in Walkington, who suggested he should go to see John Huzzard, a farmer, who also lived in the village and was a Beverley Rural District Councillor.

Having broken the news to Doris and had his tea, Ernie got out his bike and rode to Walkington, where he knocked on the door of Broadgate Farm. Caenwyn, John Huzzard's wife, answered the door and in reply to Ernie's request to speak to her husband said he had fallen asleep after being up all night tending his incubators. However when Ernie told her what he wanted she asked him in and woke her husband. After a reviving cup of tea Ernie repeated his request to swap houses with

Walt Sissons and having checked on Ernie's ability to pay the rent he agreed to sort it out for him. He was as good as his word and he and Ernie remained good friends until his death.

Walkington was still within biking distance of the quarry and Ernie carried on working there, rising to the rank of charge hand and earning good money, but one day after 'a bit of a bust up' he walked out. It was raining but the manager was demanding dry chalk. Ernie spoke his mind, the Manager got upset, one thing led to another and Ernie reluctantly left.

Jim Kennedy, the Manager of the Beverley Labour Exchange, lived in Walkington with his wife Eileen and through him Ernie soon got another job as a storeman at Armstrong's factory in Eastgate in Beverley where Doris had worked and just behind his parents' home in the Old Friary. It was a well paid job but it was indoors and after the freedom of the quarry Doris says it nearly killed him. By now Christine and Pat had left school and found themselves jobs and one day Ernie came home and said "That's it. I'm packing it in. I'm going to work for myself. I'm going to go back to the beginning and be a jobbing gardener."

Doris was less than thrilled by his decision, taken without consulting her at all. There were still bills to pay, still four mouths to feed and although she now had a part-time job it wouldn't keep them all. They had no savings, Ernie had no equipment and if it rained a self-employed jobbing gardener didn't get paid. So had he given any thought to what he would do if he couldn't make a living? Doris says emphatically "No!" Ernie just grins and sayd 'he'd have thowt o' summat'. He adds proudly that he has never drawn a penny of dole money in his life.

His first job was with John and Heather Crooks at Northgate House. John was a Veterinary Surgeon in Beverley, formerly assistant to 'James Herriot' in Thirsk. Ernie was also employed one day a week to tidy up the churchyard. Gradually he found more jobs as his availability spread by word of mouth, then he bought a rotovator and advertised his services.

New estates were being built in the village and he saw a potential market for 'bottoming' new gardens. Although he didn't drive, Colin 'Cocky' Drew, a close friend who worked as a welder for R B Massey's of Market Weighton during the week, would drive him around at the weekends. Ernie bought an old ambulance from Mark Burgess of the Icecream shop. He'd bought it originally for seven pounds but sold it to Ernie for forty. It was all black with 'one-way' windows - you could see out but not in and Ernie and Cocky became known as 'the undercover kids'.

They found plenty of work in Walkington and the neighbourig villages of Cherry Burton and Bishop Burton and they worked hard, only knocking off for Cocky to have a 'roll'. He persuaded Ernie, who had never smoked, not even in the army, to join him and eventually Ernie was hooked and started asking Cocky for one. He was then told to buy his own!

One job they were asked to do was to rotovate a new orchard at a big house in Walkington, getting as close to the trees as possible. The owner was away on the day they went to carry out the work and they decided to 'make a proper job of it'. They dug out all the trees and stacked them to one side then rotovated the whole area and replanted the trees. The owner was delighted, said they'd done a good job and paid up. He wasn't quite as delighted the next spring when he found he had mixed rows of apples, pears and plums when he thought he had segregated them!

There was plenty of work, clearing new gardens and laying down lawns and if they had been ambitious enough and had more capital Ernie thinks they could have built up a proper landscape gardening business, but Colin was unwilling to give up his steady job and Ernie was never a 'hungry fighter'.

One thing that did develop was the job in the churchyard. He was asked to take out all the kerb-stones surrounding the individual plots and stack them ready for sale, level the graves which were raised above the surrounding area and make it possible to use mechanical equipment to keep it tidy. He was to go on working there for thirty years and to include grave digging amongst his duties.

Ernie eventually worked in the gardens of many Walkington residents and despite his seventy plus years still has several clients on his list. Content to keep his head above water financially it has left him free to follow many other pursuits. His disinterest in actual hard cash has also led to some hilarious and wonderful adventures.

# Chapter 12

## PERKS

The Barter system of payment is alive and well and living mainly in the villages of Yorkshire! I know of a school which accepts remuneration for pupils' fees in bales of hay for the resident ponies. As far as Ernie is concerned money has never been of great interest to him. Riches are counted in a different coin - the beauty of a summer morning, a garden in bloom, a well-grown bed of onions, steak and kidney pie and the love of wife and daughters. So when payment for an hour, a day or even a year's work is offered in kind he is more than likely to accept. This acceptance has led to some hilarious adventures in which the hapless Doris has inevitably been involved.

Take the time he was offered a cruise on a luxury yacht in return for services rendered to a very wealthy gentleman. Ernie had been involved with 'Mr. M.' for a number of years, laying out his garden and providing all manner of services, both practical and advisory. When Mr. M. moved away from the village he invited Doris and Ernie to tea, to see his new home and to offer them a 'holiday of a life-time' cruising in the Mediterranean on the luxury yacht '*Suvretta*'. They accepted, and were told to be ready by the following Monday morning when they and their luggage would be collected.

Mr. M. arrived in his Jaguar with his wife and two children and they set off for the airport. Ernie was very impressed by the luxurious car - until a front tyre blew out on the A1. It frightented him to death and proved to be an omen for the journey. The flight to Naples was relatively uneventful except for Ernie inadvertently leaving a leather brief-case, entrusted to him by his host, on the plane. Unbeknown to him it contained a large amount of cash - 'spending money' for the holiday. He was told he must go back for it, so he set off at a run across the airfield, waving his arms at the Comet air-liner as it prepared to taxi along the run-way. The startled pilot brought the aircraft to a halt and Ernie bellowed his request for his 'left luggage'. Fortunately for him - and his host - it was found and hurled from the door onto the tarmac, to be retrieved by a grateful Ernie and handed back to its owner.

Once cleared through customs 'Mr. M.' decided that two taxis were needed for the party and their luggage and directed his guests to 'take that one and follow us'. Although Ernie speaks fluent French his Italian is almost non-existent, but he managed to indicate to the driver that he should 'follow that cab'. Where to he had no idea. He swears that there were at least ten lanes of traffic along the route taken by Mr. M.'s taxi and inevitably they soon lost sight of it. 'Where to?' became of vital importance. Ernie tried miming a ship, but as far as he could gather the driver thought he meant a train. Eventually after exchanging a great deal of voluble and incomprehensible Italian and broad Yorkshire they somehow arrived at the harbour, where at least they knew the name of the yacht. So, apparently, did everyone else and they were soon re-united with their host.

Once on board they were escorted to their luxurious 'en-suite' quarters by the bearded Captain, who informed them that he was theirs to command. This was to be their holiday and they could choose where they wanted to go. Ernie demurred. He was, he said, only a poor working man. This brought a frown of displeasure to the Captain's face and Ernie was told in no uncertain terms not to talk like that. It would do no good, warned the Captain. The rest of the guests were toffs but they respected money. If asked Ernie should say he was 'in wool' in Yorkshire. Otherwise he shouldn't refer to his status, just enjoy being a VIP.

Next morning the weather was glorious. The yacht was still riding at anchor in the Bay of Naples and Doris and Ernie emerged onto the deck to find tables laid for breakfast and waiters hovering ready to fulfil their every whim. Ernie's whims ran to bacon, eggs, sausages, kidneys and all the trimmings. But when it was laid reverently before him a most peculiar sensation came over him. He of the iron constitution felt sick! Doris too felt queasy and by mutual consent they retired to their cabin. Much concerned Captain and crew kept enquiring after their welfare and offering a variety of food and drink and also insisting that they should choose their destination.

Eventually they recovered sufficiently to confess that what they would dearly love to do would be to call on "Our Gracie" in her home on the Isle of Capri. Gracie Fields had spent a good deal of her childhood in the village of Walkington with her relatives, some of whom still live there, and Ernie wanted to pass on some personal messages. To his delight, not only did the Captain agree to his request, he said he could land them at Gracie's private beach. Some further nauseous hours later he did just that, anchoring off Capri and ferrying Doris and Ernie to the island in the yacht's elegant speedboat, instructing them to 'wave when they wanted to return'. Looking back at the yacht way out in the bay Ernie had his doubts about the efficiency of the plan but was too delighted to be on dry land to really care!

Once on the island they found themselves by a swimming pool surrounded by tables and chairs so sat down while they considered their next step. Peering through the throng Ernie could see a path leading up to the house and with his usual belief in the direct approach declared his intention of 'trying his luck'. He marched up the path and knocked on the door which was opened by an Italian servant. In his best Yorkshire Ernie explained that he would like to see Gracie to give her a message from Walkington. The flunkey was singularly unimpressed and firmly closed the door.

A dejected Ernie returned to Doris by the pool-side and in his usual dulcet tones recounted his lack of success. At the next table sat an elegant Italian lady who happened to understand - and speak - English. She asked whether he had come ashore from the *Suvretta* and when he confirmed it, she asked him to explain to her what he wanted then disappeared towards the house. In no time at all the Italian menial poured himself down the path and implored Doris and Ernie to do him the immense favour of following him back to the house. There they were met by a short square man who held out his hand and introduced himself as "Boris-Gracie's husband". Ernie explained his mission and, ignoring the captain's advice, reiterated that he was 'only a working man.' "So am I," said Boris, and recounted the story of being called in to repair Gracie's television and staying to become her husband. He also said that Gracie often spoke about Walkington and although she was out shopping he was sure she would be delighted to see them if they could wait.

So they did, and she was, hugging and kissing them and insisting that they spent the rest of the day there, catching up on news of England, and especially that small part of East Yorkshire which held so many happy memories. Boris even produced his own favourite remedy for sea-sickness which worked wonders and after a delightful stay Ernie "waved" to the yacht and to his enormous surprise the speed-boat immediately roared across the water to collect them. Their last sight of Gracie and Boris was as they waved them goodbye from the balcony of the house.

Next stop for our intrepid sailors was Ponsa. They arrived just as dusk was falling and tied up in a scene of pure enchantment. The whole island seemed to be strung with coloured fairy-lights which glowed and sparkled against a velvety sky. A gentleman in a pure white tuxedo appeared on the dock-side as if by magic. Coming aboard he introduced himself in halting English as the Italian owner of the local night club and three of the restaurants. Still suffering from mal-de-mer Doris and Ernie were glad to accept his invitation to step ashore and dine. Ernie couldn't catch all that was said in the introduction but later gathered that it was intimated that if these two VIP's from the posh yacht were happy with their treatment they might well bring twenty or so of their well-heeled friends to join them on the following day. They certainly had no complaints about the meal, or the refusal to let them pay, and with pledges of undying friendship and a wealth of extravagant Italian gestures they took their leave and made their way back to the *Suvretta* for the night.

Next morning they again went ashore, deciding to avoid the town and head instead for the beach where they intended to swim. When they arrived, clutching their swim-wear discreetly rolled in their beach-towels, they were a bit surprised to find all the pairs of golden bodies lying glistening in the sun were male. This was apparently the favourite spot for the rich Italian men to bring their English boyfriends. Seeing their hesitation a local inhabitant came to their rescue and in halting English explained they would be much happier walking along to the next bay, just beyond the rocks. There they could quite simply plunge in. They soon found out what he meant. As they rounded the rocky outcrop they were met by a golden-haired golden-skinned beauty clad, in Ernie's words 'in just a few drops o'watter'. She was being enthusiastically pursued by a bevy of young men similarly unattired. So what did our towel-clutching duo do? They shed their clothes and quite simply 'plunged in'.

Feeling decidedly better after a day in rather than on the sea Doris and Ernie settled down for the night in their cabin as the *Suvretta* sailed for Elba. Unfortunately a mistral blew up and the travellers soon realised that they hadn't really known what sea-sickness was until now. At one point as they heaved up and down, rolling and pitching in the fierce wind, Doris asked Ernie if he knew where they were. All he could see through the porthole was dark green water, churning and swirling, and expressed the opinion that they were on the way to Davy Jones' locker and as far as he was concerned it was a good job too as he was fed up of being sick! They did eventually reach Elba - and inevitably another adventure. They tied up cheek by jowl with a number of other 'floating gin palaces'. On one was Matt Busby, Manager of Manchester United, on another a heavily guarded Aristotle Onassis. Plus, of course, their guests.

Next morning Ernie noticed a procession approaching the yacht in the adjacent berth - an entourage of heavily armed body-guards surrounding a dark-haired and voluptuous beauty wearing enormous dark glasses, presumably to counteract the blinding flashes from the diamonds adorning her person. "That," said Doris knowledgeably, "is Maria Callas." A young acquaintance of Ernie's expressed a strong desire for her autograph. "Well ask her," was Ernie's advice. The young man, quite naturally, was a bit reluctant. Miss Callas had by now disappeared on board along with most of her "friends," but that didn't put off our Ernie. "Come on,"he instructed, and set off up the extremely long gangway towards the single armed man remaining at the top. The young autograph-hunter was no light-weight and as he and Ernie made their land-lubbers' way up the virtual suspension bridge it began to sway alarmingly. "It's meant to do that to deter visitors," declared Ernie, but his young friend had had enough and retreated hastily to the safety of the quayside. But not Ernie.

Clutching the rope hand-rails he hauled himself up to the top and respectfully addressing the guard as "Sir" he greeted him cordially. The response was not encouraging. "You - funny man - go away." Ernie could see that there was a language difficulty so slowly and patiently and with appropriate mime he explained that his young English friend desired Madame's signature. This obviously made an impression because the guard indicated that he would ask 'the boss' and sauntered along the deck to do just that. The portly figure sitting in the padded chair under the awning put down his drink and his paper and lowered his sun-glasses a fraction to inspect our hero standing modestly at the top of the gangway, then decisively shook his head. The guard sauntered back, relayed the refusal and repeated, "Now - funny man - you go."

For once Ernie admitted defeat and returned with some difficulty down the swaying link between yacht and quay. It is one of the few times that he hasn't managed to achieve his mission in life - acquiring for other people those things that they are too timid to ask for themselves.

What he really wanted for himself and Doris at that point in time was relief from sea-sickness. It had become quite obvious to everyone that the original plan to cruise on to the Greek Islands was going to cause Ernie and Doris a great deal of distress. Their sea-sickness was getting worse rather than better, a fact Ernie put down to 'nerves' as he had frequently travelled by sea before without suffering anything more than a slight queasiness. Whatever the reason, decisions were taken in high places and the Captain declared that if they were to enjoy the rest of their holiday it would have to be at anchor and where else would a luxury yacht feel at home than Cannes, in the South of France. So they put to sea for the last time and tied up in the exotic playground of the rich and famous.

Doris and Ernie enjoyed their stay in Cannes. They did all the touristy things, including visiting Nice, Monaco and the Casino at Monte Carlo, where Ernie wagered - and lost - his ten bob as he marvelled at the fortunes which changed hands all around him. As they came out Doris decided to immortalise the visit by taking a photograph of Ernie sitting on the Casino steps. No sooner had he arranged himself artistically than two security men approached him and explained kindly but firmly that 'it wasn't allowed'. Ernie of course asked, equally politely, 'why?' They said because they said so and what was he going to do about it. Ernie drew himself up to his full height, looked them squarely in the chest and said he was going to go. Doris in the meantime had calmly taken her photograph.

The holiday of a lifetime was nearly at an end, but there was one more treat in store. To make up for the places they hadn't been able to visit they were flown to Paris for a day's sightseeing. They were met at the airport by a hired car and driven around

*The "Suvretta", our yacht!*

*Ernie with Gracie Fields in Capri in 1965.*

*Ernie and Doris in Cannes.*

*Ernie, Doris and friends in Nice.*

*Ernie and Doris in Paris, under the Eiffel Tower.*

the city to all the famous buildings before being flown back to Cannes. From there they and their hosts were to fly back to England but when they arrived at the airport they were told that due to an air-traffic controllers' strike there were no available seats. It was here that Ernie, by now somewhat blasé about money and what it could buy, was amazed and appalled by its power.

Four seats were miraculously freed on a plane about to leave for England, to the impotent fury of their rightful occupants. A somewhat embarrassed Ernie and Doris boarded the plane to find that their allotted seats were scattered rather than together, and Ernie found himself next to an attractive Brazilian lady. When the drinks were served he accepted his miniature bottles but promptly put them into his pocket rather than pouring them into his glass. His astonished companion demanded to know why he had done that. He explained yet again that he was only an ordinary working man, that he had been given a marvellous holiday and that as it was most unlikely that he would ever experience anything like it again he was taking the bottles of spirits as souvenirs. Once again his instinctive openess paid of. The lady was impressed and not only gave him her drinks plus gifts of cigarettes and perfume but demanded that fellow passengers did the same. A fitting end to a memorable fortnight.

Contrary to expectation, Ernie and Doris were in fact to have another wonderful holiday abroad, fortunately with no sea travel involved. As a self-employed jobbing gardener Ernie worked half days for many of the village householders in the area. One morning in the early 1970's a car pulled up as he was pruning a client's roses and a fresh-faced young man got out and introduced himself as Dr. Kenneth Sugars, a newly arrived resident. Ernie thought he looked too young to be a doctor and of course, said so, but despite that he agreed to add him to his list.

After some while Dr. Sugars told Ernie that he was thinking of giving up his Beverley practice to join the Royal Navy. He hoped his wife and children would be able to join him once he got settled, so would Ernie be able to keep the garden tidy and keep an eye on the house? Agreement was reached and for the next two years Ernie faithfully carried out his part of the bargain, neither asking for nor receiving any remuneration. But home on leave Ken Sugars came to see him to settle up, offering payment either in cash or kind. He was by then stationed in Gibraltar, living in married quarters in a detached house in the town itself. His suggestion was that

114

Doris and Ernie should join them for a fortnight, all expenses paid, an offer which was enthusiastically accepted and in May they took off from London airport.

As they approached The Rock an announcement by the captain urged passengers who hadn't landed in Gibraltar before not to be alarmed by seeing the sea on either side and in front of them at touchdown, or by the sudden reverse thrust of the engines. There was terra firma beneath the wheels he assured them - it was just rather limited. Flying low over the Spanish mountains Ernie had been astounded at how high up the vineyards grew and was still marvelling over this as they landed, to be met by Dr. Sugars resplendent in the gold-braided white uniform of a Surgeon Commander.

The mornings of their holiday were to be free to do as they wished, the afternoons and evenings - and even far into the night - being reserved for a variety of entertainments laid on by the hospitable doctor and his wife. Ernie and Doris revelled in their surroundings. The May weather was glorious and the bird-life especially interesting to Ernie. He noticed as soon as they arrived that the usually brash pigeons were very nervous and soon discovered why. A pair of Peregrine Falcons were nesting on the cliff immediately behind the house.

His host organised an early morning bird-watching expedition for him. He met his guides, three Cambridge-educated Gibraltarians, at 3.00am under a lamp post in the main street. They drove up the rock as far as possible then started to climb on foot. At about a thousand feet above sea-level not only did Ernie's legs give up but the proximity to the cliff-edge unnerved him. He felt a compulsive desire to dive down, down into the sapphire blue sea. However, safely seated on a rock, he marvelled at the view and at the birds. Golden Eagles soared around him on passage from Spain, temporarily secure in this haven where shooting is banned. The youngsters still had enemies however. The local seagulls would drive them into the sea where they drowned, although Gibraltarians rowed out to rescue them whenever possible.

All around the Rock the migrating birds are at the mercy of the shotgun-crazy Europeans who shoot anything that flies. According to Ernie during the migrating seasons there is a gun 'every yard' in Malta and the Italians massacre seventeen to eighteen million birds every Spring and Autumn. Across the border the other way in Spain it's nearly as bad.

Keeping a respectful distance from the Barbary Apes and the edge of the cliff Ernie thoroughly enjoyed his day on the Rock. Meanwhile Doris was appreciating the shops full of embroidery, being warned by the friendly Indian shopkeepers not to buy when the cruise liners were in port, as all the prices were trebled on those days. When the *Canberra* put in, Ernie and Doris braved the waves for a trip in a small boat out into the bay to see her at close quarters.

They sampled the local restaurants, where Ernie was delighted to find 'good English food - not foreign muck!' including wonderful fish and chips at Sweaty Betty's, whose title misled him into thinking it was a 'knocking shop.' They found the residents very pro-British and very friendly but thought they took the local beauty for granted.

Ernie and Doris never tired of sitting on the balcony of their hosts' house from where they could see across the border into Spain in one direction or watch the sun set over Morocco in the other. One thing that intrigued them was the series of huge iron rings set into the cliffs. They were told that right at the top was a gun weighing three hundred and fifty tons put there by the British to defend the Straits. It had to be hauled up by hand, and was tied to each ring as it went to give the men a rest. The rock itself is riddled with miles of tunnels where the residents could shelter from the bombing of later wars, but Dr. Sugars estimated that many of the original tunnellers must have died from the effects of inhaling the dust as the passages were blasted and dug by hand.

Another spectacle Ernie also cast an expert eye over was the Changing of the Guard and he visited the cemetery where the dead from the Battle of Trafalgar are buried. Local legend has it that when Nelson himself died he was first brought to Gibraltar and put into a barrel of brandy to preserve his body until it reached England and that the brandy was subsequently drunk by the thrifty sailors! Unfortunately when Ernie visited the cemetery it was sadly neglected. Soldiers and sailors from many countries and centuries were buried there and he felt that there should be an international group set up to oversee its care.

The entertainment laid on by their hosts in the afternoons and evenings took many forms. There were barbecues and parties most days, many of them carrying on into the small hours. Vast quantities of huge steaks and gallons of 'Horses' Necks' (cheap brandy mixed with wine) were consumed. In Ernie's opinion the latter 'knocked your head off' and his fellow guests 'supped a helluva lot'. Never a heavy drinker he would give up and retire long before the end of the parties and sleep the sleep of the just.

More in his and Doris's line was the 'state visit' to HMS *Norfolk*, a brand new cruiser which docked a couple of days after they arrived. Dr. Sugars engineered an invitation for them to vist the ship as guests, which posed a sartorial dilemma for Ernie. Knowing the weather would be warm and that they would be staying in a private house and mindful of the weight restrictions on the flight he hadn't packed a suit, just sports jacket and flannels, not acceptable for such a formal occasion. Sue Sugars borrowed a suit from a colleague of her husband's but unfortunately the trousers were too short even after Doris's most skilful efforts. But it was that or nothing.

They were piped aboard a ship lit up overall to find the officers lined up to meet them. The Captain greeted Ernie as the 'Walter Gabriel of Ken's village' and enquired why his trousers were at half-mast. Feeling a 'proper Charlie' Ernie explained, the ice was broken and they enjoyed their visit immensely.

They were shown over the ship and Ernie was amazed that unlike in his strictly disciplined days in the Guards everyone was on first name terms and everyone 'mucked in' and did their share. The Captain and Officers had in fact prepared the deck for the party and Ernie had a few words to say about 'lax methods'. Not lax, returned the Captain, on a modern fighting ship teamwork was essential. Every member of the crew was a highly trained technician and in such a closed community they had to work as a 'family unit'.

An extra pleasure on that wonderful evening was to meet a nurse from their neighbouring East Riding village of Cherry Burton, rounding off yet another unforgettable experience.

The two holidays were exceptional forms of payment but over the years Ernie has received many small acknowledgements of his work including a sheepskin coat and a number of Savile Row suits. Fortunately they were from someone of similar stature who was off to live in warmer climes. What Ernie has given in return is impossible to quantify but I'm sure that all his clients are happy with their part of the bargain.

# Chapter 13

## SHERIFF OF WALKINGTON

Ernie and Doris and their two little daughters moved to Walkington in 1949 while Ernie was still working at the quarry in Queensgate. On moving day he went to work as usual but asked Herbert Jameson, the crane driver, to watch out for a Watts' removal van with Doris and two little girls dressed in red sitting in the front and to give him a shout when he saw it. Herbert duly did and Ernie knew that that night after work instead of turning right into Beverley he must turn left and cycle to his new home in Walkington. That was the start of whole new life and ultimately of several new careers which were to lead him to fame if not fortune.

Although the council house they moved into wasn't a palace it was new. The previous tenants had been short of cash so hadn't been able to afford much in the way of decoration. The composition floors had been painted black to save on floor coverings and it was all 'a bit rough'. The back garden was still just a field. But if she *had* been asked whether she wanted to move there then Doris would have said 'yes' as the Highgate house, although renovated since pre-war days, was still dark and old-fashioned and still had no bathroom.

If Doris had found Beverley quiet after London she was to find Walkington even quieter. The girls, then aged six and four, took to it straight away, enjoying the atmosphere of the little village school, but for their mother 'shopping' in a village without a proper shop was a new experience. There was quite a good bus service into Beverley because of it being on the route for Broadgate Hospital but in an emergency that didn't help. Like the time she ran out of potatoes.

Although there wasn't a 'proper' shop certain things could be bought from Miss Farrow's house. Doris knocked on the door and asked for a pound of potatoes but was told she didn't sell them. However, said Miss Farrow, she would give her some. Doris was astonished. She had never met with this sort of kindness to a total stranger before.

There were other things to come to terms with as well. They had a small paraffin heater and one day when Ernie was at work it ran out of oil. There was always somebody to tell you where you could get things and Doris had been told that Disraeli Gardham ('Dizzy') who lived in a cottage at the back of the pond dispensed paraffin to the villagers so taking a small bottle she knocked rather hesitantly on the door and asked for 'a pint of paraffin please'. Dizzy was a daunting looking man with a big moustache and when he roared "What?" young Doris took fright. However she stood her ground and repeated her request. He was highly amused. He'd never before been asked for a pint, he only dealt in gallons, but he filled her little bottle and refused payment. The story of course soon went round the village with the added comment "Bye, we've got a mean b . . . . here!"

When Doris and Ernie moved into their council house only forty-four had been built in the village. They quickly made friends with their semi-detached neighbours Alan and Florrie Collingwood who had been in a month, not knowing then that they would live next door to each other for over forty years. On that first evening Ernie

117

noticed that Alan and Florrie kept chickens so after dinner he took the vegetable peelings round for them to boil up for chicken food. Later that same evening Alan and Florrie came round to see if any help was needed in moving furniture and so began a long and deep friendship.

All the newcomers to the estate had young families and as they dug their gardens and decorated their houses they all quickly became friends. Alan and Florrie had three children, Ernie and Doris two and Harold and Vi Collinson six so joint outings were fairly boisterous affairs. None of them had any spare money so expeditions to the countryside around the village had a dual purpose. They collected fallen branches which they sawed up in the evenings for fuel. On summer days at the weekend they piled the children into prams and walked across the field behind their houses to 'Fishponds' and Risby Woods where there was a ruined cottage whose orchard yielded apples, pears and plums. Moor Cottage had been damaged during the war by a land-mine intended for the gun-emplacement located nearby, part of the battery of anti-aircraft guns trying to protect the city of Hull.

They also knew where to look for eggs laid by straying chickens and there were mushrooms and brambles aplenty in season. The pram bottoms would be filled with this 'free' food to be shared out when they arrived back home.

One day when they were going through Walkington Cover, a wood on the edge of the estate, they came across half a dozen rabbits hanging from the branch of a tree. They were still warm. Doris was pushing the pram with the little girls in it so Ernie lifted them out, popped the rabbits in the bottom and the girls back on the top. Next evening he met the under-keeper, Arthur 'Fonce' Dearing, who greeted him with 'Bye they're a mean lot of b . . . . s up your way on the housing estate aren't they?' He then told a story about Fred and Tom Wassling letting sparrows out of his hawk trap at one end of the wood while his mate stole his rabbits from the other. He'd been getting a dozen together for the Little Weighton British Legion supper. "What do you think of that?" he concluded. "Lowest of the low Arthur," said Ernie piously.

Once a year the whole village went on an outing to Bridlington. It reminded Ernie of the stories his Granny used to tell him of village outings when she was young and which were to lead to his most famous idea in years to come. But in the early fifties he was content to just enjoy them with his young family. Organised by the Sunday School six coach-loads of villagers would spend a day by the sea with all the children being given half a crown to spend.

The newcomers weren't really accepted by the older residents for a long time. Apart from the resentment which council estates invariably aroused in those days the incomers were not considered to be proper country folk having moved from the metropolis of Beverley! Doris had the additional disadvantage of being a 'foreigner' who didn't speak the local language but talked 'Londonish'. There was further resentment when she successfully applied for the post of the very first 'canteen lady' at the old village school. There were mutterings about 'favouritism' and 'pushy newcomers' but Doris stuck it out and helped to serve dinners in the village hall for nine years. She had already built up quite a thriving little business making dresses to order and was accused of 'wanting it all'. She specialised in wedding outfits and never needed to advertise, her expertise spread by word-of-mouth being sufficient to keep her busy.

Ernie too was 'getting his feet under the table'. In 1950 Bethel Taylor, headmaster of the village school, asked whether he and his pal Bill Taylor would be willing to serve on the Parish Council as they were two members short and no-one had volunteered. Ernie's Dad advised him against it, warning that if he disagreed with any of the councillors they would throw him out of his house. "You know what you're like," he added shrewdly. "You'll open your mouth and say anything without thinking."

Ernie however accused his Dad of still living in the medieval era with its feudalism and harking back to his boyhood when he'd had to touch his cap to Lord Hotham in the Estate village of Holme-on-the-Wolds. "World War Two stopped all that Dad," he told him and joined the Council. Again it was to have a long term effect on his life, lasting more than forty years and continuing to this day.

Ernie's particular friends in the village were Tom and Fred Wassling, brothers who worked at the quarry, Colin 'Cocky' Drew and Bill Taylor, plus of course Alan Collingwood and Harold Collinson. He was quickly introduced to the delights of the Risby estate which abutted the village on its southern boundary. As well as the primroses and bluebells beloved of his youth it brought opportunities for a renewal of his less innocent pursuits such as poaching, 'but never with a gun' he adds in mitigation.

One snowy Sunday Colin Drew called for him with his Alsatian and Ernie borrowed Alan's Jack Russell terrier Floss. The quartet set off for Risby woods to dig out rabbits to supplement their meat ration. (Meat was one of the last things to be released from rationing after the war.) Having dug out half-a-dozen and put them in a bag they decided to hide them under a bush while they penetrated further into the wood, then collect them on their way home.

They had dug out quite a good few more and Colin had his head down the hole pulling another out when Ernie remarked laconically that they had 'gotten company'. Fonce Dearing was standing under the trees at the edge of Briar Pit some fifty or sixty yards away watching them. He had his ferrets in a bag and a gun over one arm. He came across when he saw that he had been spotted and said he was going to 'pinch' them as he had caught them red-handed. He had also, he said, found their cache. He was 'shouting and cursing like keepers do' but Cocky was in no way abashed and offered him a 'roll'. He accepted, and gradually quietened down, saying if they promised not to come again he wouldn't prosecute. Ernie readily promised but Cocky refused.

When asked why he said, 'because he wasn't a b - - - - - liar like Ernie was!' Fonce threw their rabbits at them in disgust and they made their way home. Despite this encounter Cocky went back the same afternoon 'to finish the job!'

Ernie had great respect for Fonce. He had been a keeper before he was called up and served in the RAF Police in Italy. His father-in-law, 'Old Man Charles', was head keeper on the Risby Estate and according to Ernie 'one of the best keepers in England.' Peter Clapham, now head keeper on Dalton Estate, got his training there. The Risby land had belonged to Captain Arthur Wilson-Filmer, a descendant of the Wilsons of Tranby Croft who part-owned the Ellerman-Wilson shipping line and hosted the infamous 'Baccarat Scandal' house-party. Captain Wilson-Filmer never prosecuted Walkington lads for poaching or trespassing, but wouldn't tolerate the use of guns and his game-keepers had orders to confiscate all fire-arms.

Ernie appreciated the peace and beauty of Walkington after the traumas of the war and at last began to settle down and 'get his head together.' He had also learned a few lessons in respect of his council duties. He remembers somewhat ruefully that he had embarked on his civic career 'like a knight in shining armour, mounted on his snow-white charger, like a Don Juan tilting at windmills'. Not for him the wheeling and dealing, the lobbying and mutual back-scratching. He was going to play it straight, no names no pack-drill. His fellow-councillors, quite predictably, resented this up-start shooting his mouth off.

Serving at that time were farmer Fred Richardson, who was also a Rural District Councillor; farmer and landowner Staveley Stephenson; Jackie Dunning; Eileen Kennedy; David Garside, clerk to the Council; Dolly Dickinson; Lorna Mackenzie and Ted Lear. The Chairman was headmaster Bethel Taylor who had recruited Ernie. Our hero soon found his halo becoming bent and tarnished as he learned the subtle difference between corruption and compromise and that unless they all pulled together they wouldn't get anything done. He did however 'stir things up a bit', persuading more villagers to stand for the council, which generated more interest through the necessity for elections. Ernie would tour the village with Colin Drew in a loudspeaker van urging the residents to vote, trying to involve the increasing number of newcomers in the life of their chosen community.

The powers of a Parish Council are mostly persuasive. In the 1950's one of the things they were responsible for was street lighting. As there was very little, they had to install it - not without opposition. They also gave the initial 'yeah or nay' to local planning applications, which then went forward with their recommendations to Beverley Borough Council. The Parish Council Chairman was elected by his fellow-councillors - Ernie has held this office several times since he was first elevated in 1978, including his current spell which started in 1986. He also served as a County Councillor for three years.

A Parish Council is unique in that it is open to the public. Any resident can put a question or air his views through the Chairman, unlike the Borough Council, where you have to speak through your councillor and are not entitled to speak at meetings. The Parish Council also has to hold a 'Parish Meeting' once a year, usually in March in the case of Walkington. In the past this has resulted in some lively evenings with a full village hall and a good deal of humour.

One day Ernie received a phone-call from a member of the British Council asking whether they could bring a party of foreign students for an evening visit to 'a typical East Yorkshire village'. He of course agreed, and set about making hospitable plans. The students were based at Endsleigh College in Hull, brushing up on their English, and were of many different nationalities, but the first coach-load were all American.

The villagers were waiting to welcome them, headed of course by Ernie. He boarded the coach, and bade them welcome. When they enquired who he was, in his usual restrained way he told them he was the Sheriff of this one-horse town who got paid for shooting miscreants and for burying them as well. This went down very well and he was soon nick-named 'The Sheriff'. Subsequent coach-loads of varying nationalities - Chinese, Japanese, Portuguese or whatever - received the same initial welcome before being split up into pairs to be hosted by the villagers.

One evening the party consisted of Mexicans, Argentinians, Chileans, Japanese and Brazilians. A Brazilian and a Japanese girl, 'a bonnie pair of lasses', were assigned to Ernie and Doris, and he took them into the Dog and Duck pub for a drink

*Sheriff of Walkington!*

*Verger Ernie, officiating at the wedding of Gillian Collinson,
daughter of his friends, Harold and Vi.*

before cutting them a bouquet of flowers from various gardens where he worked as he walked them to his house in the moonlight. The Japanese girl was wealthy, the Brazilian not so, but they all got on well and they both addressed him as Sheriff. He was glad they appreciated the joke. At least, he thought they did.

Two or three years later Ernie and Doris received a parcel from Brazil. In it was a school text-book used throughout the country for the teaching of English. One exercise was an account written by a Brazilian student of her visit to Shakespeare's country where there was a town with a lake on which there were swans and ducks. There they met a man who was a real live Sheriff who was paid for killing people and burying them. There was even an illustration of Ernie.

The story of the 'real-live Sheriff' spread like wild-fire and the national press soon got wind of it. They requested a 'photo-opportunity' by the pond, but when Ernie arrived he found a big horse-box parked there containing a huge white horse. Now mythical white chargers are one thing. Real live four-legged beasties are another. Although the Sheriff agreed to wear the 'dudes', complete with star, Stetson and guns, he declined to change from infantry to cavalry. Nevertheless the resulting 'fast-draw' was syndicated throughout the country and many people still call him the Sheriff to this day. What the Brazilians think of English village life isn't recorded.

The Parish Council does have some funds. In the 50's and 60's one fifth of a penny per pound of rateable value was levied and once a year a Finance Meeting is held to decide how much they will need for the coming year. Currently they spend between twelve and fourteen thousand pounds a year and they apply to Beverley

Borough Council for that amount. However, this money is for essentials, not for special occasions.

Ernie was Chairman of the Council in 1978, the year of the Queen's Silver Jubilee and responsible for many of the celebrations, but in 1953 he was a relatively new member as the village prepared to mark the young Queen's Coronation. It was his first introduction to 'begging for money', knocking on the doors of comparative strangers to ask for donations. By 1978 he was an expert and at a special Parish meeting it was decided that each child should be given two Jubilee coins and a commemorative mug. Retired villagers would be treated to a three-course lunch at the Ferguson Fawsitt pub in the centre of the village. One lady, when asked by Ernie for a contribution, told him to come to her last and if he was short of his target she would make it up. She subsequently wrote him a cheque for two hundred and fifty pounds, just one of the many acts of generosity by residents over the years.

When Ernie and Doris moved into Walkington in 1949 they were delighted that their house backed onto the village 'cricket pitch', a rather rough rented field with a cricket square in the middle but precious little else. A magnificent row of ancient beech trees divided it from the new housing estate and gave the crescent its name - Beech View. The Reverend Tony Lawrance, rector of All Hallows, and headmaster Beth Taylor were keen to develop it but the cause wasn't universally popular. However a committee was set up to run it and Trustees appointed, among them Ernie, and this was to lead to many of his more famous exploits, chronicled in a later chapter. Many years later he was to serve in a similar capacity on the board of the Sherwood Trust which was instrumental in providing a site for a village bowling green.

After looking after the churchyard for many years Ernie became further involved with the church. As mentioned earlier he was first asked to 'tidy it up' in his capacity as a jobbing gardener. Once a year in June or July year the Reverend Tony Lawrance used to organise a workforce to scythe the grass and nettles which by then were three to four feet high. The 'hay' would be stacked into cocks which local farmer John Foster would then cart away.

When the new incumbent, the Reverend Leslie Reynolds came he decided that a concerted effort was needed to make maintenance easier. It was he who asked Ernie to take out the kerbstones and level the ground so that a mechanical mower could be employed and the churchyard kept permanently tidy.

Leslie Reynolds was succeeded by Michael Burdon, a former Beverley Grammar School teacher who had resigned his post to take holy orders. Walkington was his first parish. Still a young man he was a very different kind of rector from the previous two Ernie had worked for. Although at first somewhat taken aback by his views the villagers eventually became very fond of him and were sorry to see him go.

When he had been in the village a week he called on Ernie and told him he would like to offer him a lighter job. As an old soldier Ernie was immediately suspicious. The 'lighter job' was that of Verger but Ernie said he would be no good as he couldn't guarantee to be available on Sundays. As a self-employed gardener he had to take work whenever it came along, whatever the day of the week, but the rector explained that that wasn't what he required. The Church Wardens took care of the Sunday services. What was needed was someone to be available during the week for weddings and funerals. As he was already taking care of the churchyard and helping to dig the graves it would merely be an extension of his duties and on that basis Ernie agreed to take the job.

His duties include putting out the 'staddles' to support the coffin during a funeral service, lighting the candles, putting out the correct hymn books or service cards, putting the heating on in winter and generally making people feel welcome. Often, particularly at weddings, the congregation is drawn from many parts of the country and Ernie thinks it is important that they are made to feel at home in a strange church.

The first time he was called upon to officiate it was a 'double date' with one wedding in the morning and the other in the afternoon. The morning collection was decidedly thin and the rector suggested that instead of just leaving the collection plate on the table by the door Ernie should stand and hold it. Ever one for doing a job properly he not only held the plate but made a few suggestions to the departing guests as to the size of their donation. Whilst most took it in good part and church funds were boosted in a most satisfactory way he was reported to the officials of the York Diocese and that particular fund raising idea was nipped in the bud.

At another wedding the bride, overcome by the occasion, fainted on the chancel steps. Ernie grabbed the half bottle of brandy hidden away for just such an emergency and rushed up the aisle. Unfortunately he tripped and with a diving tackle worthy of an England forward he took the rector out of the field of play. Disentangling himself the reverend gentleman was heard to mutter that if anyone was in need of brandy it was him.

Although Ernie doesn't attend church regularly he is quite clear about his own faith. As a student and lover of wildlife since he could toddle he says he doesn't need a parson to tell him that there is a creator and maintains that the annual migration of birds is the greatest miracle of all. He learned to pray during the war when fear made even tough Coldstream Guardsmen ask for protection from a formerly discounted Deity and he has continued to say his prayers nightly. He considers it a privilege to be able to 'help old friends on their way' by officiating at their funerals and helping to dig their graves. Having enjoyed their companionship during their lifetime he thinks it fitting that he should be there to say farewell. Inevitably as he gets older he finds that the churchyard becomes increasingly filled with his friends.

On a less sombre note he has been equally privileged to prepare the church for the weddings of many of his friends' daughters as well as those of his and Doris's own two daughters and their granddaughter and he has taken pride in trying to make things 'really nice' for their big day.

# Chapter 14

## THE VILLAGE

During the last few years we have visited dozens of villages in East Yorkshire and even before we came to know so many people in Walkington we not only felt welcome but thought it had a more typically village atmosphere than any other. This is no doubt due in no small way to the numerous activities which take place and which owe their success to the hard work and co-operation of so many of the residents. To write about them all would fill an entire volume - and maybe eventually will! For now we will have to content ourselves with looking at just a few of the more spectacular events of the last forty years.

In 1950 it was decided to revive the popular pre-war sports and fancy-dress day, which had lapsed during the hostilities and never been restarted. Colin Drew, Dick Grantham, Tom and Fred Wassling, Alan Collingwood, Bill Taylor, Walter Dixon, Cliff Cooper, the Reverend Tony Lawrance, headmaster Beth Taylor who agreed to be treasurer and of course Ernie, who was appointed secretary, formed a committee to organise the event. The Reverend Lawrance was in the chair and they were fully supported by their wives. The three acre field had just been purchased from Captain Arthur Wilson-Filmer's Risby Estate for two hundred pounds, half of it donated by Beverley solicitor Max Dunning in memory of his father and it was this first sports day which gave Ernie his grounding in fund-raising techniques as he accompanied Walter Dixon and Alan Collingwood on a tour of local farmers asking for donations. The event, the first of many, was a great success with all the village children taking part and being followed by a dance for the grown-ups in the village hall in the evening. It also led to Ernie and Bill Taylor being invited to join the Council.

In the mid 1950's the Playing Field Committee appointed a Board of Trustees to administer the funds being raised. Ernie was one of the original board, a post he still proudly retains. The aim was to equip the field with tennis courts, a children's play area and a pavilion. Fund-raising had been going on for some years with 'Aunt' Sarah Richardson running garden parties and others organising jumble sales and coffee mornings, but it was decided that something on a bigger scale was needed to generate more money quickly. In 1958 St. Nicholas' Church in Beverley organised a barbecue at England Springs. This was a relatively new craze imported from America and some of the Playing Field Committee went along to see how it was done. They were quite impressed but decided they could do it better.

Ernie offered his services as organiser of that first Walkington barbecue, which was to take place on a Friday evening in July 1960. There was no 'kitty'. Everything was ordered in the hope that enough money would be taken to at least cover expenses. Ernie had ordered three hundred and fifty bread rolls from the Rambla Bakery where he had once - briefly - worked, and Ted Lear, Chairman of the organising committee, was to buy coconuts for the shy from Humber Street.

Friday morning dawned wet and as the day went on it got wetter. Dozens of helpers in macs and wellies were poised ready to erect tents and side-shows. The Rambla Bakery rang for a decision. If they put the rolls in the oven they would have to be paid for. "Stick 'em in," said Ernie defiantly. Ted Lear wanted to cancel it, saying he wasn't going to get the coconuts. Ernie said he'd better or Dick Grantham who was running the shy would be using Ted's head! Everybody was already soaked to the skin and morale was at rock bottom. The weight of opinion was in favour of cancellation but Ernie obstinately refused to give in.

At 5.00 o'clock he rang RAF Leconfield and asked what hope there was of a break in the weather. None, they said, there wasn't a gap in the clouds in any direction. At 5.30 the rain stopped, the clouds parted and the sun came out. But it had already made the conditions underfoot well-nigh impossible. The only entrance to the field, not at that time tarmacked, was a quagmire. Bill Taylor, Ernie Herdsman and Fred Wassling sped off in a van and mysteriously 'acquired' a load of gravel which they tipped into the eight-foot (only later was it widened to a ten-foot) just in time for the arrival of the first guests.

The sausages that evening were cooked on open braziers - forty-gallon oil drums with holes punched in and filled with burning coke. Hull Brewery ran the beer-tents and the main event of the evening was a tug-of-war between the village team, Hull City Police and various Rugby teams. The village had a plentiful supply of big men and the village 'bobby', PC Dempster (last year's Mayor of Pocklington), suggested the idea. Dick Pinder, another Walkington resident, was a tug-of-war expert, and he coached the village team. He had at one time pulled for the Palestine Police.

Walkington won the tug-of-war contest on that memorable evening, Ernie's neighbour collapsing on the rope with excitement. Their success inspired Ernie, who immediately began to prepare for the following year. By chance he saw in a copy of the Daily Express an article about a tug-of-war team called Outwood Farmers. It was led by a huge man called Bill Nixon who had seven sons. He only needed one more for a complete team! He boasted that they were the finest team in England. They came from Cheshire, and Ernie wrote to him and said they might be the best in England but not if you included Yorkshire! Bill Nixon turned the letter over, wrote 'Name place and date' on the reverse and posted it straight back to Ernie. It was the start of a wonderful series of events.

In 1961 Outwood Farmers came to the Walkington barbecue. A cattle-truck drove onto the field and when Ernie enquired whose it was he was told it was their opponent's anchor-man who was so big it was the only way he could travel! Bill Nixon said to leave the draw to him - he would arrange it so that Walkington met Outwood in the final.

There were between two and three thousand people present that night to see the final pull. Outwood Farmers let Walkington pull them nearly to the mark then Bill Nixon said "Right - tek 'em!" And they did. The Playing Field Committee had provided a Championship Cup and Bill Nixon filled it and drank a toast to 1962 when, he said, he would arrange to bring some of the best teams in the country to join in. He was as good as his word and Bill Taylor's young daughter Anne who lived opposite Ernie said they ought to have a personality to present the cup. On being asked 'who?' she suggested Elsie Tanner of Coronation Street, the Granada Television soap opera, who was currently at the height of her popularity. Ernie has always been grateful to young Anne for her suggestion. (She grew up to be a Sergeant in the Hull City Police Force but still calls Ernie 'Mr. Teal'.)

Ernie wasted no time in writing to Pat Phoenix, the actress who played the part of Elsie, to ask whether she would be the guest of honour at the 1962 barbecue. Three nights later when he was in the Barrel Inn with some friends the landlord, Sid Oxtoby, told him he was to go home. Doris had rung to say he was wanted on the phone. He was indignant. He didn't often go to the pub and thought Doris was just using the phone call as an excuse to get him home. However when he arrived it was to find that Pat Phoenix's secretary had rung and he was to return her call before 11.00pm. He did and she said Pat had agreed to come as it was in aid of the playing field for the children and that there would be no fee.

When Ernie had written initially he had promised that if 'Elsie' agreed to come he would send a Rolls Royce to collect her from Manchester with 'the best driver in England' at the wheel and she said she would hold him to that promise. Ernie wrote next to the Editor of the Daily Mail and told him about the efforts of the Playing Field Committee and that Elsie Tanner would be at their annual barbecue and would be presenting the tug-of-war cup. He ended his letter by saying "However I don't suppose a national paper like yours is interested in what we are up to in this far-flung corner of England."

Next day the phone rang. It was the editor in person wishing to speak to Mr. Teal. He said he had actually screwed up Ernie's letter and thrown it in the bin, but that final sentence had rankled and he had fished it out again. He was going to send a reporter and a photographer and would Ernie arrange for the tug-of-war team to be ready to have their picture taken.

When the reporter arrived he confirmed the editor's story of the retrieved letter, wrote his story, took his pictures and left. There were various reactions to the finished article which appeared the next morning. The first was from Dick Pinder, the team's coach, who was appropriately enough away on a coach tour and not therefore included on the photograph. He was furious. Not at his exclusion but at the fact that the team line-up 'looked like a dog's hind leg'. Second was the village reaction to the assertion that the team ran down to the sea at Bridlington every morning for a dip as part of their training regime. Ernie as usual had been gilding the lily and the reporter had believed him. Finally the publicity given to the event guaranteed a turn-out at the barbecue which very nearly daunted even Ernie. But not quite.

The 1962 barbecue was the biggest event ever staged by the little village of Walkington. The Daily Mail having warned them that the presence of Elsie Tanner would bring thousands flocking to the ground the committee requested two large beer tents from Hull Brewery instead of the usual small one. Eight thousand sausages and eight thousand bread rolls to contain them plus a hundred loaves, three hundred and fifty chickens, two calves and four lambs were ordered to feed the estimated five thousand and more. To help with the preparations Chris Jeffries, chef at Broadgates, cooked the lambs and calves in the hospital kitchen ovens overnight. On the actual day Clarice Scotter arranged them on spits to make them look as though they were being roasted on the spot. The police came to the ground the day before to advise on crowd control and approve the single vehicular entrance. Even the weather co-operated. It was a beautiful day.

Ernie's neighbour, Alan Collingwood, worked for R. B. Massey in Market Weighton and he had asked his boss if he could borrow his Rolls Royce for the evening. Mr. Massey had generously agreed and Alan arranged to pick up Pat Phoenix from the Granada Studios in Manchester at 6.00pm. He was warmly welcomed by the actress who introduced him to her fellow cast members before they set off on the long drive back across the Pennines. Alan had left Walkington at 3.00pm and arranged to telephone Ernie's house, where Harold Collinson would be waiting to receive the call, when he reached Market Weighton on the return journey so that the officials could be waiting to welcome her.

By 8.30pm there were eight thousand people on the field and another two thousand still trying to get in. A chant started. "We want Elsie." They weren't interested in PT displays, tug-of-war contests or brass bands. They had been promised Elsie Tanner and that is who they wanted - NOW!

By a quarter to nine Chairman Ted Lear was becoming excited with worry and the odd soothing pint so when Harold Collinson came to tell Ernie, who was standing next to Ted, that the car would be there in ten minutes Ted lost his bearings. Pointing to the side entrance to the field he said to Chief Inspector Maidment who was in charge of the Police contingent "She's coming in there." Thirty policemen and their complement of dogs rushed to the entrance by the church and proceeded to push back the crowd.

Ernie was convinced that the original arrangements still stood - she would be entering by the eight-foot. Over the Public Address system he asked all tug-of-war men to rally to him. One hundred and fifty heavyweights, all dressed in their team colours, obeyed the call and they forced their way to the entrance. Eddie Fryer, the County Librarian, was still there with his two tables taking the entrance money. He already had over a thousand pounds in two shilling pieces - a considerable weight. On being told he must move he very reasonably asked where to? Bill Rice, Beverley's famous huge be-whiskered singing policeman, hadn't time to argue. He picked up Eddie and his money and dumped them over the wire fence into the nearest garden. The jammed eight-foot was cleared in the same way, the first person to suffer the indignity being the rector, the Reverend Leslie Reynolds.

Elsie meanwhile had arrived at the entrance in the Rolls to find a melée of people trying to fight their way in but no officials or police. Her manager told Alan Collingwood to drive on, but at that moment Ernie and Bill Rice emerged like corks out of a bottle. Elsie got out of the car, the tug-of-war men surrounded her clutching a complete circle of rope and she entered the field. The crowd went mad, seeing her with her long auburn hair and wearing a red trouser suit they flocked like moths to a candle. Men went down like nine-pins, but the ring of tug-of-war stalwarts stayed firm.

It was difficult to make progress towards the centre of the arena as the crowd surged around them and they found themselves being pushed inexorably to the left where Bill Taylor and his wife were dispensing tea from a stall. Ernie realised with horror that with his back to them Bill was unaware of what was happening and that any minute now he and his tea-stall would be trampled under-foot. At the last moment the crowd veered to the right and eventually they were in the arena. Elsie addressed the crowd over the loudspeakers and persuaded them to settle down and watch the final of the tug-of-war, again between Outwood Farmers and Walkington and again with the same result. She presented the trophies and was then escorted to the old wooden pavilion in use at that time. It was flanked by two wooden pay boxes where tickets were bought to be exchanged for hot-dogs. These were soon surrounded by the crowd and they and the pavilion were in danger of collapse. Again

*The Tug-of-War Team at the 1960 Barbecue. They defeated the East Riding Police in the Final.*

*Back row, left to right: Norman Castle, Alan Collingwood, Ron Bradford, Dennis Gray.*
*Front row, left to right: Dave Witty, Dick Grantham, Dick Pinder, Tom Waslin, Cliff Cooper.*

*Pat Phoenix, "Elsie Tanner".*

*Pat Phoenix's husband, Alan Browning, who accompanied her to the 1965 Barbecue.*

130

*"Elsie Tanner" with village children in 1965.*

*"Elsie Tanner" and bodyguards at the Barbecue.*

Elsie appealed for calm and again the crowd eventually settled down.

A light supper had been prepared in the pavilion for the VIP's, including wine, and having consumed it Elsie said she needed the loo. Unfortunately the old pavilion didn't include 'conveniences'. These had been set up behind the beer tents, which were on the other side of the field. A suggestion that the thirty policemen and all the tug-of-war teams should be re-assembled to escort her through the crowds was rejected. The situation was too urgent! There was a small room off the one they were in and she enquired what was in there. She was told it was for visiting cricket teams and had a light but little else. "That'll do," she said, "if you've got a bucket."

Ernie and Dick Pinder stood guard on the door as Elsie retired, but within a minute she started to scream. 'Rats', guessed Dick Pinder and he and Ernie charged to the rescue. But it was humans that were the cause of the screams, dozens of them with their noses pressed to the curtainless windows as Elsie squatted on the bucket with her trousers round her ankles. Ernie and Dick tore off their coats and covered the windows, their backs tactfully turned until Elsie regained her clothes and her composure. A more status-conscious star might have been put out, but not Pat Phoenix. She was very down-to-earth and a good sport and she and Ernie got on 'real well.'

Before she left, this time in a Jaguar, she signed autographs at a shilling a time to swell the proceeds even further. Alan Collingwood drove her back to Manchester, where he stayed the night at the home she shared with her mother. The evening had taken thirteen hundred pounds of which eight hundred and seventy pounds was profit, a staggering amount in those days.

The aftermath was decidely a back to earth situation. The playing field was a mass of paper rubbish and, what was worse, broken glass. A team of volunteers, mostly women, worked across it on their hands and knees picking up every fragment. What also became clear was that if they were to cater for that number again the oil-drum braziers would have to be replaced. They looked picturesque, but the fumes made the team of fifty helpers tending the frying sausages and onions quite ill. A little 'industrial espionage' came up with a design for bottled gas ovens,being perfected by Beverley Lions for their annual barbecue and Bill Taylor of Top House Farm, a blacksmith by profession, set about making four of them, each capable of holding two hundred sausages at a time. Made out of old bedsteads and cast-iron plates they were a resounding success and are still in use.

Elsie Tanner returned several times to grace the annual barbecue, a couple of times staying overnight in the village and visiting housebound residents the following day. Always considerate, when Ernie suggested a visit to the 'Fergie' for a drink before she went home she pushed two ten pound notes into his hand saying she knew he couldn't afford to pay, thus saving him the embarrassment of her paying for him in public. On the night of the barbecue she always walked right round the edge of the arena so that people could shake hands with her and on that first occasion had stopped to talk to a little spastic girl called Linda Drew. After that she would always ask after Linda and Linda in her turn would always be enquiring when Elsie would be coming again.

Although Pat Phoenix never asked for a fee the organising committee bought her a present and made enquiries as to what she would like. The cast of Coronation Street were at that time helping to support a home for spastics at Sale in Cheshire and whenever they were offered gifts would choose a vacuum cleaner, an eiderdown or some other item suitable for use in the home and this is what Pat did. As an extension of this she asked Ernie whether he and the tug-of-war team would put on a tournament at the Home. They took two bus-loads and had a wonderful day out as well as raising funds for the patients.

The tug-of-war team eventually assumed a life of its own beyond the annual barbecue and the team travelled all over the country to national tournaments and county shows and even to Broadmoor Hospital. One of their first engagements was a return match with Outwood Farmers whose leader, Bill Nixon, was a wealthy man, owning seven or eight farms. He hired an entire public house for the night and had a huge copper full of stew waiting for them at his farm. He even loaded them up with bags of pies and pasties when they left.

On one occasion they were taking part in a tournament at York Racecourse sponsored by Summer County Margarine. Resting between bouts Ernie listened with interest to the running commentary being broadcast over the public address system. It was, he decided, rather good. Never one to stint praise where praise is due he located the commentary box in the centre of the arena perched high on scaffolding, climbed the ladder, stuck his head through the door and said, "I don't know who you are but you are the best tug-of-war commentator I've ever heard."

He went back down the ladder and told PC Bill Rice of the East Riding Police Team, also taking part in the contest, what he had done. Then he looked in his programme and read the credits. 'Commentator Wynford Vaughan Thomas.' Unabashed he returned up the ladder, apologising for not recognising him but repeating his congratulations.

The team twice reached the finals of the National Championships which were held in London at White City. This meant a coach trip and an overnight stay which was booked by Cocky Drew through R. B. Massey's of Market Weighton where he worked. The first year they stayed at the modestly priced Kenilworth Hotel. Although the team didn't do very well, being paralysed by nerves on their first big occasion, the weekend was a great success.

The next year the Kenilworth couldn't take them and Colin booked them into the Hotel Russell which he said was 'only a bob or two dearer'. It took some finding as it seemed to be surrounded by 'No Entry' and 'One Way Only' streets but eventually Colin, who was driving, drew up at the door. They were all a bit surprised to find a squad of uniformed 'flunkies' who eyed the motley crew somewhat askance. However they were guests, they were booked in, so they pounced on the luggage and led the way inside. One of them didn't quite manage to conceal his expression of disdain as Jock Rankin handed him his paper carrier containing his heavy 'pulling' boots and emblazoned with the slogan 'Eat Peck's Fish and Chips. They're Good For You.'

When the booking was made they had been asked to submit a list of names so that rooms could be allocated. As the list of travelling supporters had not at that time been finalised Ernie had used his imagination. So when the receptionist enquired which were Mr. and Mrs. Hood, Ernie pointed to two stalwart members of the team and said "You Cliff and you Ernie." The receptionist's eyebrows rose as she asked whether he was sure. On being told 'yes' she was heard to mutter something about 'peculiar people up in Yorkshire' but eventually they were all sorted out.

Some of the team's supporters had never been away from home before never mind stayed in a high class hotel in London and in some cases it went to their heads. It's difficult enough for most of us to know how to behave in a strange situation but for some of the older villagers it was totally bewildering. Walt Easton was found by Ernie next morning tucking into his breakfast without jacket, collar or tie but wearing his flat cap. Mrs. Ida Gillyon, an elderly lady who had worked hard all her life and brought up a large family of children loved travelling with the tug-of-war team and they loved having her. She had rarely left the village before and when she saw a group of Arabs in the hotel in their spotlessly white flowing robes she asked if there was a fancy dress party.

When they took her for a trip on the Underground they had already taken the precaution of putting a label with her name and address and the name of the hotel round her neck and another round her wrist and everybody had been urged to keep an eye on her, but somehow in the rush to get on the train she was left behind. When they discovered she was missing they all piled off at the next stop and Ernie caught the next train back. Fortunately she was still standing on the platform obeying instructions 'not to move'.

They took her round Picadilly Circus and to Buckingham Palace which she instantly recognised as the 'King's house'. It is difficult to tell who enjoyed it more, Mrs. Gillyon or her escorts as all the tug-of-war team loved Ida!

Several of the younger element in the party decided to sample the night clubs and restaurants of the capital and again their inexperience let them down. Some got away with a hangover but Dick Grantham and his friends fell foul of the oriental powers of persuasion. They had already had a jar or two when they went into a Chinese restaurant and ordered a meal. After they had eaten Dick, who had done the actual ordering, was presented with the bill which came to seventeen pounds and ten shillings. He queried it and was told that it was 'very reasonable'. Unfortunately he misunderstood, thinking it was just for his meal and he became abusive, enforcing his argument by grabbing the waiter by his pig-tail. Other waiters materialised as if by magic and despite their superior size and weight the lads were forcibly ejected. Sobered by their experience they hailed a taxi, Dick expressing the opinion that he never wanted to see another Chinaman as long as he lived. His wish was not granted. The taxi-driver was most definitely oriental!

Next morning, nursing their collective headaches, the party prepared to move out. Cliff Cooper took Ernie aside and said thay had a confession to make. They had forgotten to book a room for Cocky Drew, the driver of the coach, so Cliff and his room-mate had tied their single beds together and Cocky had shared with them. Unfortunately the beds hadn't been up to the combined weight of three stout tug-of-war pullers and in Cliff's words 'a bolt or two had come loose!' The dilemma was, should they just sneak out and pretend nothing had happened, or should they confess? And if the latter, would they have to pay for the damage?

Ernie said they must report it and they returned to the room and rang for the maid. She said it looked O.K. to her, but when they both leaned on it, it collapsed. She was appalled - nothing like that had ever happened in the hotel before. Ernie slipped her a pound note and she agreed to report it as an 'accident.'

Before returning home the coach party went to Petticoat Lane, where again unfortunately the inexperienced Northerners were taken in by the expert stallholders and paid over the odds for a variety of unsuitable presents to take home, including a 'scarf' which was in fact a table-runner. Then they visited London Airport to gaze in wonder at the huge airliners taking off and landing, finally driving home at the end of a lovely day.

It wasn't, however, quite the end of the saga. When the bill for the weekend arrived from R. B. Massey's the 'bob or two' that had been predicted as the extra for the hotel turned out to be more than three times the previous year's charge. Everybody owed another four pounds ten shillings - a week's wages in many cases. They were advised by a village resident who hadn't been one of the party not to pay. It was, he said, obviously a misunderstanding and a big company like Massey's would never take a little village tug-of-war team to court.

Ernie took the advice and declined to pay the extra money. With hindsight he admits he was wrong. He should have paid up. The company had always been good to the village, lending cars, allowing them to use the workshops and supplying materials. But the damage was done. One day while he was working in a client's garden he was served with a writ - a County Court Order. Fellow Parish Councillor Dolly Dickinson now advised him to go and see Mr. Massey and throw himself on his mercy. She would accompany him she said, as she was a friend of them both.

When they arrived in the office in Market Weighton Dolly was immediately asked by Mr. Massey to 'keep out of it,' as it was strictly business between himself and Mr. Teal. He then put it to Ernie that it was him who went to the solicitor first, it was him that refused to pay the two hundred pounds, and that it was him - not the club - who would have to pay not only the bill but the costs of any court case. He was, he said, hurt that Ernie hadn't come to him in the first place and explained the situation when they could no doubt have come to some arrangement. Now he wanted his pound of flesh. Ernie could do nothing but admit that he had been wrong and agree to pay up, but it was the end of a long friendship.

After years of staging the barbecue and running the tug-of-war team it was decided to try something new, and for a few years a 'Pageant of Pubs' became the annual event. Quizzes were also run, contests between the different new estates going up in the village in the forties, fifties, and sixties, and they have carried on to the present day. Sunday Galas were popular for a year or two, organised by Mrs. Farr, the doctor's wife, all day affairs involving PT displays, marching bands and the Holderness Hunt. They have given way in recent years to car boot sales, held once a month from May to October and a very lucrative source of funds.

The village pond has been central to the Christmas celebrations for many years, but it wasn't always so and the Bowling Club is a relatively new venture as well. But the major project being undertaken even as I write this is the building of a new village hall. In all these events Ernie has played and continues to play a decisive role, but as he and his contemporaries age other, younger residents are happily coming forward to shoulder the burden. Theirs is another story and must wait for another book. We must return to our main theme - the life and times of George Ernest Teal and his family.

# Chapter 15

## THE CELEBRITY

It all started with a robin called Gutsy. Ever since he had toddled alongside his Granny Railton as she collected kindling on Beverley Westwood in the 1920's Ernie had loved the birds. His job as a gardener meant that he had time to study them even more and to become friends with the 'regulars' who came to feed in the gardens where he worked. Always noted for their partiality for humans who obligingly turn up worms for them one particular robin who lived in Margot Ingram's garden at Sherwood Cottage lost all fear of Ernie and slowly and patiently he taught it to take food from his lips. The magic moment was captured by the camera and the resulting photograph was circulated first to the local press and then to the Nationals. Ernie quickly earned a reputation as 'the naturalist'.

In 1971 BBC Radio Humberside, newly hatched itself and on the look-out for 'human interest' stories soon got to hear about him and Ernie's broadcasting career was launched. During the last twenty-one years he must have filled many hundreds of hours with his home-spun wisdom, his tales of the countryside and his comments on the world as he sees it. From four minute up-dates on the seasons to hour-long chats about his life and his activities he has a devoted and vociferous following. If for any reason he is absent from the air-waves for any length of time the letters pour in asking why.

Recently the pattern has changed a little. As well as the regular monthly short 'out and about' features which I have the pleasure of recording with him and which as I write are currently broadcast on the weekend breakfast shows we have recorded a few 'holiday specials'. In the summer of 1991 we spent an hour chatting about his early life and playing some of his favourite music. For the first time Doris joined in to tell her side of the story.

In the spring of that year and again at Christmas he was involved with others, introducing listeners to some of his favourite people. In the spring it was Brian and Sylvia Baldwin who have set up a small but remarkable Nature Reserve in Holdernss and Ernie and I spent a wonderful afternoon talking to them and playing some of *their* favourite music.

At Christmas we visited a primary school on the outskirts of Hull and Ernie talked to the children about Victorian Christmases and Doris showed them examples of the kind of clothes the Victorians wore. Then the children asked them questions about Christmas when they were little and played and sang carols for them. The resulting enchanting programme made a magical start to Christmas Day.

In the past many members of Radio Humberside's staff have been involved with Ernie - Paul Heiney who was the producer of Ernie's first broadcast about the village pond; Jim Latham, the station's News Editor, who lived in the village and was Chairman of the Hayride Committee in the 1970's; Margaret Henriksen, a teacher seconded to Radio Humberside for a year; and in more recent times Charlie Partridge, a devoted admirer, and Martin Plenderleith who has spent many happy hours with Ernie on Beverley Westwood.

Over Easter 1992, in anticipation of the Silver Jubilee of the Hayride, we visited Geoff Morton and his heavy horses to find out more about these gentle beasts, the resulting programme being broadcast on Good Friday. Ernie also appears regularly as a guest on the Countywide Phone-in when listeners can ring in and consult him personally on countryside matters.

His broadcasts soon brought many requests for him to talk in person to Women's Institutes, Luncheon Clubs, Young Farmers' meetings and charity functions and he is still in great demand often with three or four engagements in a week. As his popularity has increased so the list of societies inviting him to their functions has broadened to include Rotary; Inner Wheel; Free Masons; the British Friesian Society at the Gimcrack Rooms at York Racecourse where he has been twice; Trade Associations and Old Boys' Dinners. It was at one of these that he almost - but not quite - took offence.

Eric Mackman rang him and asked whether he would reply to the Toast to the Guests at a Hull Old Grammarians' Dinner - the annual celebration of past pupils of Hull Grammar School. He agreed without realising 'how big a job it was'. When he arrived it was to find three hundred and fifty guests including a fair sprinkling of VIP's. There were two other speakers besides Ernie and he was to be the final one.

After they had eaten there was a brief interval to replenish drinks at the bar and visit the cloakroom and when Ernie returned to his seat he found a large piece of card on his plate on which someone had written 'Mr. Teal, please do not forget that My Lord Bishop is present'. Somebody had obviously been spreading rumours about Ernie's colourful language and slightly risqué stories.

The first two speakers were, in Ernie's opinion, brilliant, which increased his nervousness, already heightened by the censorious message. His neighbour, seeing his worried expression, tried to cheer him up. "Last year," he said, "we had Sir Leonard Hutton. I found him boring. Hope you're not going to be!"

Ernie rose to his feet. He had all his 'opening bits' ready - "My Lord Mayor, My Lord Bishop etc. etc" - then began his speech.

"Muhammad Ali always said a boxing ring is the loneliest place to be in the entertainment world. I don't agree. There are two people in a boxing ring - three if you count the referee. Where I'm standing there's only one, and that's me. I don't know anybody in this room, but somebody thinks he knows me." He then held up the card, read out the message and continued, "I won't forget my Lord Bishop. If he wants to go to the bar and get a pint of ale I'll willingly pay for it!" The assembled guests roared their approval and the success of Ernie's speech was assured.

He has never conquered his 'first night nerves', no matter who his audience is, but he has enjoyed his years on the speaker circuit. He regrets not writing down a list of the places he has visited. It would make interesting reading. He has an excellent memory for events but his favourite talks remains those about birds and wildlife while WI's have an insatiable appetite for village tales. He is so popular that he is asked back to the same venues time and time again, eventually running out of new subjects to talk about.

1976 was the year of the great drought. No-one had as yet started talking about the greenhouse effect or holes in the ozone layer but the news was filled with stories of the effects on the countryside and on industrial and domestic consumers. We were urged to 'share a bath' and put bricks in lavatory cisterns and the use of hosepipes for

*Gutsy!*

watering gardens was almost universally banned. Ernie had always contributed to the Walkington Parish newsletter but now the plight of the birds and animals moved him to write to the Beverley Guardian.

The Editor at that time was John Barratt, who lived in Westwood Road in Beverley. He was impressed by Ernie's article, came to see him and invited him to contribute a regular column, for which he proposed to pay him the handsome sum of two pounds a week. Ernie agreed and has never missed a week since, although the remuneration has increased a little.

Encouraged by his literary success Ernie gathered together some of his country-side stories into a booklet 'Hours to Share' which he had printed at his own expense and sold for five shillings a copy. All two thousand five hundred were quickly snapped up. On its cover was the now famous 'Gutsy' photograph and it covered such subjects as Colin Newlove's bull which he rode at agricultural shows, boyhood memories of Beverley Westwood and tales of his life in the Guards.

Ernie next came to the notice of the Principal of Bishop Burton College of Agriculture situated in the neighbouring village about three miles from Walkington, who asked him to talk to some of the students about birds. This was followed by an invitation to lecture to the Adult Education classes at Longcroft School and South Hunsley.

Doris was by that time also teaching at 'night school' in Beverley. After many years of dress-making locally a village resident suggested she should go to night-class and get a formal teaching qualification - her 'City and Guilds' - as her apprenticeship certificate didn't entitle her to teach.

Doris's mother had always hoped that she and her sister Gladys would set up their own salon in the West End of London but the war put an end to that dream. Now perhaps she could regain a small part of it. She passed the exams with flying colours - first class in fact - and immediately got a job at the College of Further Education in Gallows Lane about a mile to the North of Beverley town centre. For twenty-one years she caught the bus into Beverley on four evenings a week and walked up the hill to Gallows Lane or Longcroft School. She thoroughly enjoyed it and still meets former pupils in a variety of places.

Ernie on the other hand found night-classes hard work. He was a talker, not a teacher. Doris is an excellent photographer and over the years they had built up a collection of some four hundred slides of animals and birds. When he gave illustrated talks to clubs and groups she went with him and acted as projectionist. The talk usually lasted for an hour at the most, and he was happy to answer questions.

Night-classes were different. He was on his own, they lasted two hours and he had to think of a different subject each week to keep the continuing interest of the same group of students. Classes started at seven, and by about half eight he had 'run out of steam.' Doris suggested he took a slightly longer break. "What break?" he enquired. Nobody told him tea was served in the canteen half way through. The next week he suggested they stopped for tea at eight, but his students didn't want to - they couldn't get enough of him. Eventually he found it too exhausting on top of his day-time work and gave it up.

It was in 1966 that he came up with an idea which was to bring him recognition far beyond the confines of his home village - even of his beloved Yorkshire. He was to be brought to the notice of the highest in the land.

## Chapter 16

## 'WAGONS ROLL'

The idea for a Victorian Hayride began to take shape in Ernie's mind in the mid 1960's. During the previous decade he had come up with a variety of schemes to raise money for village amenities and while the majority of residents were grateful there were some who thought it was all a bit selfish. Whenever any profit was made Ernie 'grabbed it for the village'. Wasn't it time they stopped always looking after number one and started thinking about those who were less fortunate? Always one to listen to an argument Ernie applied his mind to thinking up an idea that was completely different.

His thoughts kept going back to the months he had spent living with his much loved Granny Railton when he was an impressionable little boy. She had believed firmly in the maxim that cleanliness was next to Godliness and each evening he was scrubbed down with carbolic soap in a wooden tub in front of the fire to wash away the sins of the day along with the grime. During this ordeal she would tell him stories of her childhood in Harpham, a village on the Plain of Holderness some miles inland from Bridlington.

She had left school at the age of eleven and from then on had no 'proper' holidays. Farmworkers and servants in the big houses counted themselves lucky to be given one day off a year in the brief lull after haymaking. On that one Sunday each year the farmers would clean out their wagons and the horsemen would groom the horses with linseed oil and polish the harness and brasses until they gleamed in the summer sunshine. Then they would all set off for a day by the sea. If it was too far for the horses to walk all the way they would take the villagers to the nearest railway station and meet them there on their return. Villagers from Walkington were taken to Beverley but Granny Railton travelled all the way from Harpham to Bridlington and back by horse-drawn wagon.

To while away the long journey every wagon would have a 'squeeze box' or concertina player on board and the villagers would sing along to the popular music-hall melodies of the day. When they arrived at the sea-side the women and children would spend all day on the beach, the men in the local hostelries. Women in those days never went into a public house unless they were 'common', an epithet to be avoided at all costs. In the evening everybody would be reunited for the long journey home. Experienced horses which had been hauling the wagons on the annual trip for years knew the routine and would automatically stop at every pub on the way back.

Ernie used to listen entranced by these romantic tales and they stayed on his mind conjuring up a picture of a more leisurely way of life, albeit hard-working and poorly paid. How would it be, he wondered, if they gathered together a few horse-drawn vehicles, dressed themselves up in Victorian costumes and drove not all the way to the coast but to neighbouring villages and even to Beverley, re-creating in miniature that old-time summer holiday? They could call it a Victorian Hayride and collect money from spectators and give it to charity.

Ernie mentioned his idea to a few of the older fellows in the village who shook

their heads and said he'd never be able to find any roadworthy heavy wagons. Even if he did, they said, there weren't any horses capable of pulling them that distance. And even if there were, they said, there weren't any horsemen left capable of driving them. It needs a particular skill to drive a pair of heavy horses on the land never mind on modern roads clogged with noisy traffic.

Ernie was not deterred. Once he gets an idea into his head he grips it firmly in his teeth and shakes and worries at it like a terrier with a rat until it submits. He devoted his Beverley Guardian column one week in 1966 to asking for help in setting up a ride in the summer of 1967. One of the first people to respond was Neil Thwaites, Head of the Art Department at Market Weighton School and an expert on corn dollies and country matters in general. He lives in the village of Londesborough and he rang Ernie and told him not to worry about wagons as he knew where every wagon remaining in the East Riding was located.

Neil still has Ernie's reply, dated 20.1.67.

'Dear Sir, I cannot tell you how very pleased I was to know that you were interested sufficiently enough in our Victorian Hayride to loan us a wagon. I wonder if I could come along one weekend to view it. I have now got two complete wagons with horses so we are progressing. Sir, once again please accept my most grateful thanks. Sincerely yours, E. Teal.'

On the following Sunday Neil collected Ernie in his car and they toured the local farms looking at other wagons. Neil was also a friend of Geoff Morton who cultivates his farm on the the wolds at Holme-on-Spalding-Moor almost entirely without the aid of modern machinery relying on the power of his heavy horses, many of which he has bred himself. At that time he had eighteen, but the number has increased considerably since then and Geoff has become known to thousands of people through his farm open days and through subsequent television coverage. He was 'scufflin tunups' when they arrived and his first question was what was the proposed event in aid of? On being told 'Cancer Research' he said he would willingly help and would bring two pairs of horses.

Ernie had also received information that Bradshaws of Driffield, the animal feedstuffs company, had some Suffolk Punches. He made an appointment to see the Chairman and Directors one Saturday morning and was driven there by Margot Ingram, one of his regular gardening clients, who lived at Sherwood Cottage in Walkington.

When they arrived Margot and the Chairman discovered that they had a connection in that their sons had both attended Worksop School and they were soon all getting on like a house on fire. This was all very well but eventually Ernie felt obliged to interrupt this social chit-chat to point out that what they had really come for was to borrow a pair of heavy horses. He was told not to worry they would fetch the Fetches in! This cryptic statement was the start of a long and happy association for Ernie with Jim Fetches and his brother who were expert and enthusiastic drivers of heavy horses and Jim has driven the leading wagon at the Hayride ever since.

Another firm which owned Suffolk Punches was Premier Oil Mills in Hull. One of their Directors, Michael Foster, lived at Killerby House in the village and said he would arrange for them to be made available. Not only that but they would be able to borrow them a couple of weeks beforehand for a rehearsal. They were duly yoked singly to rulleys with three tons of corn on board to simulate passengers and set out

141

to walk the ten miles from Hull to Walkington.

By the time they reached Cottingham, less than half way, they were exhausted. The corn was unloaded and they were walked slowly the rest of the way then given a good rest when they arrived at the stackyard of Northlands Farm. This was the only farm in the village with enough space in which to assemble the cavalcade and was being made available by the Waterworth family who had farmed there for generations. The route chosen for the Hayride was about ten miles but it was pointed out that it had never been envisaged that the horses would be expected to pull singly. Each wagon was to have a pair.

The trouble with this pair was that they weren't! They didn't even like each other and when an attempt was made to put them into double harness they 'went mad!' They fastened one to a gate-post while they considered the problem, but by now thoroughly disgruntled the animal sat back on its powerful haunches, lifted its head and pulled the huge post straight out of the ground. It then ran amok, kicking in the end of the wagon in passing. Doris understandably took fright and said Ernie must call the whole thing off before somebody got killed. For once he was inclined to agree. The problems seemed insurmountable and everyone was rapidly losing enthusiasm.

At that strategic moment Arnold Swales walked into the stackyard enquiring mildly whether they were 'in a bit of bother.' He asked who the horses belonged to and when told Premier Oil Mills and introduced to Michael Foster, suggested that they should break for lunch. He then talked quietly but firmly to the horse and fastened a rope round its huge neck tied with a special knot, telling it that if it started playing up again he would have it down. The horse rolled its eyes and jumped away, pulling on the rope. Down it went with a clatter and rose to its feet considerably quieter.

It was then encouraged to pull the heavy gatepost to which it was still attached back and forth, back and forth, first by itself then with its partner. Never having been paired before they were inclined to pull away from each other, but Arnold gradually got them working together, then harnessed them to a wagon and drove them round and round the field. Eventually he jumped down and said they'd be 'OK now.' It had been an anxious morning, but the Hayride was back on course.

Cancer Research had been chosen as the recipient of any money raised for several reasons. Ernie had personally lost some dear friends to the disease, research was on the increase with more hope of successful treatment and with its current high profile it was a cause with which it was felt many of the spectators would identify and sympathise. There were many arrangements to be made besides the central ones to do with the transport itself. Collecting boxes must be obtained and collectors drilled in what they could and could not do to remain within the law. It was decided to transport the collectors from village to village. The route wasn't lined for miles as it is today - indeed they weren't sure anybody would turn out to watch them.

Victorian costumes were to be optional, but obviously the more people who dressed up the more spectacular the ride would be. Mrs. Landrick, mother of Ernie's fellow-councillor Lorna Mackenzie said if they were going to do it at all they must do it properly. Vera Williams was appointed wardrobe mistress, Bill Pirrie was made Chairman of the organising committee and his wife Linda acted as secretary. Ernie of course was 'organiser'.

*A Proper Toff!*

*The Darley Dale Coach. Driver, Caroline Dales.*

*The Hayride, 1986.*

*Conducting the choir.*

Vera wrote to the Palace of Varieties show in Leeds, at that time at the height of its popularity on television. They put her in touch with Hombergs, the Leeds based theatrical costumiers. A form was included in the monthly parish newsletter asking anyone interested in taking part to fill in their measurements and what kind of a character they would like to be - milkmaids, yokels, gentry or whatever. The cost was to be two pounds per costume. Mrs Joy Albeury also borrowed some from a college where she had connections, but that first year there were relatively few actual participants. However there was a tidal wave of goodwill towards the project, even from those who thought it wouldn't work. The magic of the heavy horse was beginning to weave its spell.

Ernie himself entered another world with its own language. Although he had watched and loved the spectacle of harvests garnered by living horse-power when he was a child he hadn't really given much thought to the beasts themselves or to their equipment. Now as these gentle and magnificent animals were prepared for the big day he began to learn about swingle-trees, wide-awakes, blinders and poles. Lovely words which rolled easily off East Yorkshire tongues.

They were lucky to have the Northlands Farm stackyard in which to assemble the Hayride. It had once been called Towers Farm as there is a fine view of Beverley Minster's twin towers from its position high on the northern side of the village. It was at that time being managed by Stanley Waterworth until his nephew John, heir to the farm, came of age, John's father Alan having sadly died. Stanley and Jack Wassling were appointed wagonmasters.

Northlands farm also possessed a colossal barn and into this were brought wagons from farms scattered throughout the area. Many needed a complete overhaul with rotten wood to be replaced, wheels checked and all to be thoroughly cleaned and inspected for safety. They were after all going to be carrying a human cargo instead of loads of muck or sacks of corn. It is only now when he looks back that Ernie realises the enormity of the project he had instigated.

The safety aspect of the whole affair gave great concern to the local Police Force. While anxious to co-operate they imposed severe restrictions on how it was to be run. For example no children under the age of sixteen were to be allowed to ride on the wagons. Ironic really when a relatively short time before horse-drawn transport was the only kind available and it was the internal combustion engine which was the dangerous monster.

Ernie thought an appropriate touch would be to have a penny-farthing bicycle leading the parade. He wrote to cycle dealer Clifford Pratt of Hull who willingly agreed to lend him one. Cliff transported it to the village and unloaded it by the pond where it was received by Ernie. As he was pushing it up the hill to his house he met his neighbour Cocky Drew who asked which silly b . . . . was going to ride it. "You are!" said Ernie and thrust it unceremoniously into his hands. Next thing he knew Colin was riding it like a veteran and he led that first parade in 1967.

In that year there were only six or seven pairs of heavy horses and the Hayride was a very modest affair compared with today. Gradually over the years it has been extended to include light horses, carriages, Shetland ponies with Governess carts and traps, an ice-cream van, Ringtons Tea, even a coach-and-four as well as mounted riders and foot followers. It has always been held on the third Sunday in June and usually on a fine day.

On that first June Sunday in 1967 the horses and drivers assembled at 6.00am. Several mares had foals at foot which had to be allowed to suckle. Manes and tails had to be plaited and coats groomed until they shone like silk. The cavalcade was scheduled to leve at 1.30pm and by then quite a crowd of curious farmers and horsemen had gathered, some of whom Ernie had never seen before, diffidently offering their help as they ran their hands expertly and lovingly down the flanks of the magnificent animals.

At 1.30pm precisely the immortal words were uttered. "Wagons - Roll!" Ernie crossed his fingers, closed his eyes and prayed. They set off down the road towards the village but came to a halt as they approached the steepish hill in Northgate which leads down past the old school to the Dog and Duck crossroads. Ernie was alarmed. Had something gone wrong already? But he was quickly reassured. They had merely paused while brake-shoes were fitted to the rear wheels of the wagons so that they didn't over-run the horses as they went downhill. With sparks flying from the metal they turned left at the bottom to find a huge crowd waiting to welcome them, clapping and cheering as they made their stately progress through the village. It was, says Ernie, a most heartwarming occasion. 'Fair warmed the cockles.'

Colin Drew had chosen to dress up as a Victorian Policeman to ride the penny-farthing and he was resplendent in top hat, white trousers, black tunic with silver buttons and well polished boots. To add to the authenticity he had a whistle on a long cord around his neck and as he led the procession past the Ferguson Fawsitt he was blowing it with enthusiasm. Pride though goes before a fall. As a bevy of comely lasses cheekily blew kisses to him from the steps of the pub he let the whistle drop from his lips, bravely took one had off the handlebars and gallantly responded. Unfortunately the whistle caught in his front wheel - the big one - and as it was carried round the cord tightened round his neck and he was pulled unceremoniously over the handlebars, to the delight of the crowd. Fortunately his top hat took the brunt of the force and he remounted and carried on.

Ernie rode in the first wagon, driven by Jim Fetches and accompanied by Linda Pirrie. Doris rode on the second with Geoff Morton. There was another big turn-out to greet them on the Green at Bishop Burton and Icky Oliver accompanied the community singing on his concertina as well as entertaining the crowds with his spoon playing. They sang all the old songs, including Land of Hope and Glory which has now become a tradition. They had excellent co-operation from the police and having obtained prior permission to collect money the boxes soon began to fill.

On that first ride they went straight into Beverley past the Racecourse grandstand. In later years the traffic problems caused by the huge procession and the number of spectators have meant a change of route and the pedestrianisation of Beverley town centre eventually forced a further change in the return journey. In 1967 however there were no such problems and the Hayride made its way onto Beverley Westwood where Charlie Byass had been entertaining the waiting crowds with his steam organ. The procession stopped for another sing-song and more fund collecting then went on through Beverley Bar and into Saturday Market. As they entered the town centre St. Mary's Church clock struck four. The Hayride was precisely on time.

As they had driven into Beverley Ernie had been amazed at how many people had turned out to watch. Old men with weathered faces under flat caps had been visibly moved by the nostalgic spectacle, men who had spent all their lives with horses and who loved them for their strength and their willingness to work. All the effort had been worth it if only to see the pleasure it brought to them. By the time they wound their way through Beverley and back to Walkington some four hundred pounds had been donated and was subsequently handed over to Cancer Research. Now some twenty-five years on the total amount raised for a variety of causes is approaching two hundred thousand pounds, a figure which is sure to be substantially increased by 1992's Silver Jubilee celebrations.

As the wagons rolled back into the stackyard at Northlands Farm at the end of that first very long Hayride day the overwhelming feeling was one of relief. There was also a mood of triumph. Not only had it all gone practically without a hitch and a substantial amount of money been raised but there had been enormous enthusiasm amongst the spectators and universal demand for it to become an annual event. As the Hayriders sang Auld Lang Syne and the horsemen tucked into pie and peas ideas were already forming in Ernie's mind for the following year.

Now twenty-five years on he alone is left from the original committee and has been finally persuaded to take on less responsibility as new younger shoulders thrust up to willingly bear the burdens of this unique event and he looks forward with eager anticipation to the Hayride's Silver Jubilee.

# Chapter 17

## '. . . . AT BUCKINGHAM PALACE.'

It was while Ernie and Doris were on their 'perks' holiday in Gibraltar that the posh envelope from Buckingham Palace arrived. Daughter Christine who lives in the village had been keeping an eye on the house and collecting up the mail and when they arrived home she produced it with a flourish. Had Ernie's early days as a Guardsman caught up with him? Were they enquiring about the whereabouts of his army boots? No - it was an invitation to a Garden Party!

Four Walkington residents were invited - Ernie and Doris and Dr. Mike Scrowston and his wife Shirley, good friends of the Teals and who by coincidence had been married on their Silver Wedding Anniversary. They arranged to travel down together by train early on that morning of July 25th 1978 and went by car to Paragon Station in Hull. When they arrived Ernie found that in his excitement he had forgotten the invitations so they had to rush back to Walkington then back to Hull, by which time they had missed their train. However they caught a later one and duly arrived at King's Cross in London. Dr. Scrowston had another appointment so they arranged to meet up again at the Palace Gates in the afternoon.

A month before Ernie had written to Wellington Barracks, his old 'home', explaining that he had been invited to a Palace Garden Party and requesting permission for Doris and Shirley to be allowed to use the barracks to change into their finery. The Commanding Officer had replied in the affirmative so they presented themselves at the gate. Ernie was somewhat dismayed to find it being manned by a Royal Marine, not a Guardsman. The Sergeant of the Guard came out and Ernie explained the situation and showed him the invitation but the Sergeant said he needed proof of identity. Did he have a driving licence? He obviously hadn't heard the one about the Sherman tank! What about the letter from the Palace? Ernie pointed out that he had already given him that. "Well then," persisted the Sergeant, "could he tell him who it was addressed to?" Patiently Enie began to recite 'Mrs. Doris Teal, . . . .' "That's fine," said the Sergeant. "Just testing. Follow me."

They were led to a barrack room where Ernie found old habits die hard as he 'acquired' a fag from a packet left on a table and smoked nervously while Doris and Shirley got ready, then they all walked across to the Palace Gates to meet Mike and join the hundreds already queuing to get in. It was a beautiful day and Ernie felt as though he had come home. He was quite literally on his old stamping ground. Little had he thought as he had marched crisply up and down in front of the residence of his King as a twenty-year old that one day he would be welcomed back as a guest of that King's daughter.

Several bands were playing in the forty-two acres of the Palace grounds. Ernie spotted a couple of 1st Battalion Coldstream Guards in full dress uniform complete with rifles and after he had inspected them expressed the opinion that they were a 'bit sloppy' and that in his time their feet wouldn't have touched the ground between there and the guard-room. They in turn pointed out politely that they weren't in his time, but in their own. He had had his time. "They were of course quite right," adds Ernie ruefully.

The Royal 'cast-list' for the afternoon was the Queen, Prince Philip, Princess Anne and Prince Charles. At a Garden Party the thousands attending are discreetly herded into sections with a corridor down the middle and each Royal progresses down one corridor, stopping to speak to pre-selected guests. Ernie was determined to be in the Queen's section and they found places towards the end where the Gentlemen at Arms in morning suits and grey toppers were marshalling the crowds into place. One of these was Sir Torquhil Matheson, a member of the Queen's bodyguard, six feet eight tall and an ex-Coldstream Guards Officer. Ernie stood in his way, murmuring to Doris that he wouldn't walk past him as he was wearing his Guards' tie. Sir Torquhil certainly noticed him and asked his name.

"2658082 Teal, George Ernest." "When did you join?" "1937 - what about you?" "1944". "Why," said Ernie, "we'd got 'em beat by then!"

The ice broken they began to chat and Ernie told him about being on Palace Guard in 1938 and 39, that his Company Commander had been Lord Chandos-Pole and his Commanding Officer Lord Bingham. Sir Torquhil pointed to a group of men which included the Duke of Edinburgh who were chatting in the middle of the lawn. One of them was Lord Chandos-Pole. "If you knew him go and talk to him," he told Ernie. "You have my permission." The crowd around them had been listening to the conversation with interest and it was a very self-conscious Ernie who walked out to the centre of the lawn and tapped Lord Chandos-Pole on the shoulder. The Duke of Edinburgh looked at him curiously as he politely addressed his former superior. "You won't remember me sir but you were my Company Commander in 1938." "Was I by jove?" was the reply and they went through the 'name, rank and number' routine, Ernie adding 'same as the duck' to make it quite clear. When on request he supplied the name of his Platoon Sergeant Lord Chandos-Pole described him as 'That black-hearted b - - - - - of a Yorkshireman,' a description with which Ernie fully agreed.

They chatted agreeably for a few minutes, Lord Chandos-Pole saying that it was through the efforts of the Duke of Edinburgh that such a wide cross-section of the public was now invited to the Garden Parties and that he personally was delighted that it was so. It was like a breath of fresh air to see people like ex-Guardsman Teal enjoying the afternoon. Then he hugged him, kissed him on both cheeks (somewhat to Ernie's embarrassment) and asked if he was to be presented to the Queen. When told 'no' he said go back in line and he would see what he could do.

Ernie returned to Doris and the rest of his party in great excitement. Eventually Sir Torquhil came back with a Colonel in the Grenadiers in full uniform who questioned him about his job and about his time in the Guards. They talked about former Coldstreamers and about the death of Lord Frederick Cambridge, which Ernie had witnessed, then the Colonel said they would do their best to add him to the list of presentations but it depended how long the Queen chatted to the final guests on her list as they had to adhere to a strict timetable. "If she stays more than five minutes with them you've had it," he was told.

Several more Officers came to talk to Ernie and he had soon gathered quite a crowd around him. Eventually Sir Torquhil came back and said he was sorry but they had to curtail it. The Queen was flying to Canada that night to begin a State Visit and she must move on. He hoped Ernie wasn't disappointed.

"I beg your pardon Sir," said Ernie, "but I'm bloody disappointed! I'm bloody upset as well!" "But you must understand . . . ." began Sir Torquhil. Ernie interrupted. "Oh I do understand, but you shouldn't need to ask whether I'm disappointed not to be shaking hands with my Sovereign."

The Royals retired to the Pavilion for their tea and Ernie and Doris joined the queue for the refreshment marquee for theirs. It was, they said, a lovely tea. Inevitably Ernie lagged behind the others, chatting and observing and by the time he rejoined them their table was full. At the next table a solitary gentleman in top hat and tails was stretched out topping up his cuppa from a hip-flask. Recognising a kindred spirit Ernie asked if he could join him and was told to 'sit down - if you're feet are anything like mine you need to.'

Ernie wasn't entirely sure of the composition of the guest-list at that afternoon's Garden Party but making a wild guess he asked if his companion was a Parish Councillor like himself. "No, no," was the reply. "I'm an Admiral of the Fleet." "Oh well, you're doing a good job," Ernie assured him, not in the least put out.

Ernie and Doris enjoyed every moment of that momentous afternoon. Advised by his Naval companion Ernie paid a visit to the Royal loo to be brushed down by a uniformed attendant and on the way out through the Palace they admired the wonderful displays of porcelain. Back on the train they shared a compartment with a Swedish tourist and regaled him with the story of their day. He must have been quite bemused. They didn't come back to earth until they arrived back in their own modest home late in the evening.

One invitation to Buckingham Palace in a life-time is more than most folk can expect but Ernie and Doris were to return there twelve years later on an even more auspicious occasion. On November 17th 1989 a large important-looking envelope plopped through the letterbox in Beech View. Doris picked it up and seeing the Downing Street postmark expressed the opinion that Ernie had been fiddling his taxes again! Ernie opened it and with great excitement read the letter telling him that the Prime Minister had it in mind to submit his name to the Queen to be made an MBE - a Member of the Order of the British Empire. If he agreed would he please sign and return the enclosed form. The letter was in strict confidence and he must not disclose its contents to anyone. No further communication would be sent to him until after the announcement in the press at mid-day on December 31st.

Ernie was filled with elation. He wanted to rush out and announce it to the world but as so often in his life he was restrained by Doris with the awful warning that if he told anybody at all he wouldn't get the award. Unwilling to let his family find out the news from somebody else they decided to organise a dinner party on the evening of December 30th to tell them about Ernie's honour and swear them to secrecy until the next day. Their excuse for the party would be that it was a joint Christmas and New Year present from Doris and Ernie to them all.

Ernie walked down into the village to see his friend David Sharp, landlord of the Ferguson Fawsitt. He would like, he said, to book a table for sixteen in the restaurant on December 30th at 7.00 o'clock. "Sorry," David told him, "the restaurant is closed from Boxing Day to New Year's Day. " Disappointed, Ernie said they would make do with the carvery, but that too was closed. Seeing his crestfallen face David asked if it was a special occasion. "Very special," said Ernie. "We're treating the whole family to a do." In that case, he was told, the carvery would be opened just for them.

On Christmas Day after a few drinks it was particularly hard for Ernie not to tell the family about the coming announcement, but they persisted with the excuse that the dinner-party was just a present. On the appointed evening daughters, sons-in-law, grandchildren, brother and sisters gathered round the table and Ernie announced that Doris had something to tell them. She got out the envelope just as an attentive David Sharp came to the table to see if everything was all right. He, of course, mustn't be allowed to overhear. "Do you mind," said Ernie. "We're just about to read the family will." "What a thing to do at New Year," said David, but he obligingly withdrew and the family, when the excitement had died down, were warned that they mustn't tell a soul until after noon on the following day.

Mid-day on the 31st arrived and the more prominent awards such as Knighthoods were announced by the media. By 1.30pm he had still heard nothing officially and steadied his nerves with a double whisky. What if it had all been a dreadful mistake? What if the Queen had said 'No'? At 2.00 o'clock he had another drink. At 2.20 the phone rang. It was a reporter from the newsroom at BBC Radio Humberside congratulating him on being awarded the OBE. "No I've not," said Ernie. "It's the MBE." The reporter begged to differ saying Reuters had just announced it was an OBE and how did Ernie know it wasn't? Ernie said he'd had a letter from Mrs. Thatcher, and she wouldn't be wrong!

Immediately after the announcement was made on the radio the telephone began to ring and the efficient Doris made a list of all the people who rang to congratulate him. Next day cards and flowers arrived and Ernie was particularly pleased with those from residents of Walkington, remembering that a prophet rarely has honour in his own country. Messages came from overseas as the news spread and friends in America, Australia, New Zealand and Canada expressed their delight.

A letter arrived from the Lord Chamberlain telling Ernie he had to be at Buckingham Palace by 10.00am on Tuesday March 27th. 'Day suits' were to be worn and all expenses would be paid. He immediately went to Johnson's Outfitters in Beverley to arrange for the hire of the correct clothing - top hat, dark jacket and grey trousers. The young man who came to serve him asked what the occasion was - wedding? - christening? - a day at the races? "No," said Ernie, "I'm going to the Palace to meet the Queen." The young man had a sense of humour and having laughed politely repeated his enquiry. Ernie repeated his statement, adding that if the young man didn't want to serve him he would take his custom elsewhere. That little difficulty sorted out he was measured up and told the suit woud be ready for collection at 11.00am on Friday 23rd March. The cost would be thirty pounds.

When he arrived to collect it he tried it on and was dismayed. The trousers were 'half mast', reminiscent of his borrowed suit in Gibraltar. It was bad enough on that occasion, this time it wasn't to be contemplated. What had happened was that the poor assistant, who Ernie describes as 'a super young fella', had measured Ernie's sadly bowed legs on the straight. By the time the trousers had accommodated the curves they were far too short!

A telephone call ensured that replacement trousers arrived on Saturday and Ernie and Doris and their daughters Christine and Pat prepared to travel down to London by train on the Monday. Christine's husband John would accompany them although he wasn't invited to the actual ceremony and they would meet granddaughter Lucie and her boyfriend in London. They were to stay with Doris's brother Reg in Walcot

*Outside Doris's old home, 91 Walcot Square in London, the day before the Investiture. Left to right: Daughters Christine and Pat, Doris and Ernie.*

*After the Investiture, outside Buckingham Palace.*

Square, opposite the house where they grew up. It would be quite a family reunion.

They took a taxi from King's Cross Station and as Ernie paid the driver he asked him about ordering a cab for the next morning. He was advised not to book it that night, given the firm's telephone number and told a car would be with him ten to twenty minutes from ordering.

None of them slept that night and by 8.30am on the Tuesday they were all ready. Brother Reg, infected by their nervousness, ran out to check on the traffic in Kennington Road and came rushing back to say it was very heavy and he thought they should ring for a taxi right away. They didn't want to be late did they? He added that he didn't think Ernie should ring as they wouldn't understand him! Reg's wife, also called Doris, made the call and within five minutes the cab was at the door. By twenty to nine they were on their way and by five to they were at the Palace Gates. They had their official sticker and told the driver to go straight in but they were stopped by a policeman who on being told that they were there for the Investiture suggested that they were 'a bit keen' and that they wouldn't be allowed in for another hour. He advised them to pay off the taxi, relinquish their car stickers and go and get a cup of coffee. There were plenty of places in Buckingham Palace Road he added.

Christine was disappointed that they wouldn't be driving into the forecourt. She would really have liked to be in a Rolls Royce flying the Union Jack but would have settled for the taxi. Ernie was self-conscious in the unfamiliar togs but along with John and Lucie they set off. It was a cold morning and none of them was dressed for outdoors and Ernie was all for diving into the first café they saw but Christine refused saying they were far too dressed up. A little further along they found the Hotel Rubens and despite the tariff displayed on a board offering rooms at two hundred pounds a night excluding breakfast they went in.

Quite a few of the people milling around in the foyer were similarly attired and they surmised that they too were bound for the Palace so they found themselves a table and sat down. When they found out that coffee was two pounds fifty a cup they decided to do without but as nobody queried their presence they sat in warmth and comfort until ten minutes to ten when they made their way back to the Palace and once again walked in through probably the most famous forecourt in the world.

As they entered the Palace proper they had to walk up an enormous staircase. On each step was a uniformed soldier - Royal Horseguards and Lifeguards - with plumed helmets, riding boots, breastplates and drawn swords. At the top were a dozen Gentlemen Ushers, all in grey. Doris and the girls were led away down a long corridor, opulently furnished with glittering chandeliers and huge paintings and thickly carpeted. Ernie of course had been inside the Palace before but this was different. Then he was a young Guardsman on duty, not there to look at his surroundings but to get on with his job and do as he was told and he had only been in the Staterooms once, some fifty years before.

He was led into a huge room with about a hundred others, an Usher fastened a hook into his lapel ready for his decoration to be hung on and he was invited to be seated on a settee. He shared it with two black gentlemen and an Irishman, all as nervous as Ernie, necessitating frequent trips to the 'facilities'. Ernie estimates that he went four times, the black fellows ten and that the Irishman was 'up and down like a yo-yo!' Eventually he begged Ernie to tell him something to keep his mind off the coming ordeal and, ever obliging, Ernie told him the one about the Irishman who had

154

lessons to eradicate his Irish accent then ordered a pound of tomatoes in a fish and chip shop. Yes, that's the one! He thinks it helped because his new-found friend asked him to tell him another one.

There was much speculation about who would actually be investing them with their awards. Would it be the Queen? Or would the Duke of Edinburgh, the Princess Royal or Charles or Di be on duty? Ernie said he knew it would be the Queen as the Royal Standard was flying which meant that she was in residence and members of his old battalion, the 1st Coldstreams, were mounting double sentry. Only the Sovereign rated a double sentry and he was willing to back his assertion with a hundred pounds. A Colonel in the Lifeguards confirmed his guess as he called for them to gather round so that he could give them their final instructions. It would be the most momentous occasion of their lives he told them, as the Queen herself would present them with their awards. He said he knew that they must be nervous but that they should try to relax and enjoy it. To help them to do this he told them an improbable story about a gentleman at a previous investiture who, following on after a lady recipient, curtsied instead of bowing!

They were to be taken into the room where the investiture was to take place a few at a time and until then they were to remain where they were. For Ernie that was nearly another two hours, whiled away by chatting to others from the Hull area including one who had formerly lived in Walkington. At ten minutes past twelve a Gentleman Usher called out 'George Ernest Teal of Walkington? Right sir, follow me."

They walked along a corridor which seemed to Ernie to go on for miles. He swears it took them two or three minutes. At the entrance to the Ballroom he was handed over to another Usher who asked him if he was nervous. "Of course I am," retorted Ernie. "I'm not used to this sort of thing. I'm just an ordinary working man!"

There were about seven hundred people in the room, three hundred and fifty each side, all with their attention fixed on the Queen, but Ernie felt all eyes were on him as he walked between them on the Usher's signal after he had been relieved of his top hat and camera. He was very conscious of his bowed legs and dare not glance to left or right to locate Doris and the girls.

The next Usher led him down the left hand side of the Ballroom, past enormous pillars set some ten yards apart which impeded his view of the audience so that he was still unable to see his family. At the front he was handed over yet again, this time to an Admiral dressed overall! He told him that in a few moments he would hear his citation being read out by the Lord Chamberlain. When he got to the word Ernest he was to walk to the centre, turn to face the Queen, bow, and walk up to her, getting as close as he could to the dais on which she was standing so that she could reach to hang his decoration on the hook in his lapel. "Don't worry, Her Majesty will not engage you in conversation. She's already been standing there for two hours and is visibly tiring," he added.

The Lord Chamberlain announced 'George Ernest Teal' and repeating his instructions to himself Ernie at last stood face to face with his Sovereign. A Gentleman-at-Arms handed her his MBE and as she hung it on his lapel Ernie could see the diamonds sparkling on her fingers and smell her perfume. She straightened up and looked him directly in the eyes. Hers, he noticed, were a vivid blue, and he stood mesmerised. Then she spoke. "Now tell me Mr. Teal, where is this village called Walkington?" He opened his mouth but the only sound to come out was a strangulated stammer. Unbeknown to him Doris and the girls were seated in the front row just a few yards away and Doris nudged her daughters and said in wonder, "You're Dad's tongue-tied!"

Ernie recovered and told the Queen it was a village three miles west of Beverley. She said she had been to Beverley - it had a beautiful church. Then she asked him what he had done to earn his MBE? Once more lost for words he murmured modestly that he had 'done a job or two in t'village M'am and raised a bob or two for Cancer Research', adding that he tried to help other people as much as he could. She congratulated him and asked whether he had enjoyed the morning. This time the reply was easy. "It's been wonderful M'am". She expressed her pleasure at that and told him to carry on the good work, nodding her dismissal.

He was so overcome that after bowing he almost forgot to take six paces back, as instructed. He teetered unsteadily for a moment, came back upright, took his six paces backward, bowed again and walked away to the back of the Ballroom. There a seat had been reserved for him, an official unhooked his MBE, put it into its box and stowed it away in his inside pocket for him. He was then free to watch the rest of the investiture.

When Doris and the girls had assembled in the Ballroom they too had been given their instructions. They were to stand when the Queen entered, escorted by the Gurkhas and the Yeomen of the Guard, but there was to be no applause whatsoever throughout the ceremony. Up in the balcony the Band of the Scots Guards had been playing background music - a medley of songs from the shows - and as the ceremony came to an end at twelve thirty they too ended their performance with a flourish, the Queen bowed, everybody stood and the band struck up the National Anthem. The Queen and her escort withdrew and everybody started to make their way out. The musicians began to pack up their instruments and Ernie, ever a lover of the military band, thought they deserved some appreciation. He not only said so but began to applaud. Immediately he was flanked by two Guardsmen who, grinning, told him that was it. He was off to the Tower!

Re-united with his family they took their time leaving the Palace as they had been advised to 'make the most of it'. Ernie had already as we know availed himself of the facilities and been very impressed. He now urged Doris and the girls to do the same. "It was very nice but very old fashioned," says Doris. "Lots of solid mahogany and a lever at the side instead of a more conventional 'low flush' or even a chain - quite an experience." As they emerged into the forecourt a young Guardsman was collecting up the music stands from where yet another band had been keeping the crowds of tourists entertained during the Changing of the Guard. Ernie went up and said "Excuse me - can I carry that?" When asked why he told him that fifty years before it used to be his job and he'd like to see if they were kept in the same place. He confidently marched back into the Palace, straight to the same door to the same room, so familiar to him all those years ago. It was a nostalgically fitting ending to the morning.

Outside the Palace an official photographer was waiting and as they posed a young foreign couple rushed out of the crowd and asked if they could have their photograph taken with them. Ernie protested in his best Yorkshire that he was not a big shot, that he was of no account and lived in a council house. With great excitement they shrieked to their friends that he was a Count and lived in a Country House. Ernie gave up. "For today, I am a Count," he said.

They rounded off their celebrations with a guided tour of Wellington Barracks, which the girls had never visited before. Not that they were able to get much idea of what it had been like in their father's youth. No longer did they sleep forty to a barrack room. Now just three or four shared a centrally heated unit. But then, many things had changed. Guardsman 2658082 Teal, George Ernest, was now Ernie Teal MBE of Walkington in the East Riding of Yorkshire.

# Chapter 18

## SILVER AND GOLD

Life for Ernie and Doris as they enter their eighth decade has been filled with excitement. After the 'do' at the Palace the village staged a 'This Is Your Life' evening. For once it was a village event not organised by Ernie and miraculously kept secret from him right until the last moment.

He had been asked to speak about the investiture at a social evening in the village hall one Saturday in April. Daughter Christine said she would collect them in the car to save them the walk. It was due to start at 7.30pm and when she hadn't arrived by 7.15 he began to fret. He can't stand unpunctuality and by 7.25 he was beginning to fume about the younger generation who had no sense of timing. "We should have walked," he said and poor Doris had great difficulty in persuading him to be patient.

When they finally arrived he got out of the car to be met by a family who told him the hall was packed and they couldn't get in. Fortunately he was standing with his back to the road, otherwise he would have seen his brother and sisters arriving. As he entered the hall he was surprised to find it much more brightly lit than usual and with the stage half-way up the side instead of at the end. He couldn't see the audience because of the glare of the lights, but did notice television screens at each side of the stage.

Dennis Johnson was Master of Ceremonies and urged Ernie to sit down so that they could get on as it was late - unusual for Ernie he added innocently. He quietened the audience and said Ernie was going to tell them about the Investiture. Ernie rose to his feet and said he couldn't see them because of the light in his eyes but he would start at the beginning, on the day he got a letter. At that moment Tony Hall walked in and interrupted him. "No Ernie - not tonight. This isn't a few hours in your life. Tonight this *is* your life."

Ernie was taken completely by surprise. His daughters joined him on the stage and the reason for the lights and the television screens became clear as the whole event was videoed by an old friend, Peter Bond and filmed messages from absent friends were shown on the screens. Old friends came in and told their stories. Bob Cherry, the coach company owner, remembered their scout camp days when Ernie was detailed by the Assistant Scoutmaster to cut down some saplings to make a wig-wam. Patrol Leader Stan Warriss said, "Strike it there," Ernie swung the axe and chopped the end off Stan's left index finger. Stan fainted and Ernie nearly did. Ironically if it had been his right 'trigger' finger instead of his left he probably wouldn't have been killed in the war as he wouldn't have been in the front line.

All aspects of Ernie's life were covered, with school friends, members of the tug-of-war team and of the many committees on which Ernie has served. Mike Burdon, former Rector, sent a filmed tribute from Berwick-on-Tweed and BBC Radio Humberside's Charlie Partridge brought a recorded message from Ernie's wartime idol Vera Lynn. Wing Commander Walkington of the Walkington Society was there and of course many people connected with the Hayride. Finally a young Guardsman brought greetings from his old regiment, the Coldstream Guards. Doris received a

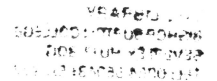

bouquet of flowers and Ernie a beautiful life-size framed photograph of himself in his formal attire wearing his medal, with a smaller one of himself and Doris as well, taken and presented by Walkington photographer Tony Baynes. The village, says Ernie, did him proud.

One of the many events covered during the evening was the presentation in 1984 of the Silver Cross of Saint George, awarded annually by the magazine 'This England' to 'a true patriot'. Other winners have included Sir John Betjeman and Margaret Thatcher. Ernie was nominated by Dr. Mike Scrowston, who also had the idea of mounting a Saint George's Day celebration in the village hall. But that again is another story for another book.

Having recovered from all that excitement Ernie and Doris started looking forward to another momentous day - their Golden Wedding, although Ernie on reflection thinks he forgot to ask Doris's father for her hand in marriage! However, the knot was certainly tied on September 23rd 1941 and they began to plan a celebration party. The guest list grew and grew until it reached a hundred and fifty and Doris began to worry about the work and expense involved. They were persuaded to abandon the whole idea and daughter Christine and the rest of the family took over.

They transformed the garage at Christine and John's house in the village with sheets hung on the walls and golden decorations, balloons and streamers. On Saturday September 21st granddaughter Julie's husband John Skelton who is a chef laid on a magnificent meal, aided by the rest of the family and friends. 'Jock' Thompson, the local piper and accordionist played and despite the drizzle Ernie and Doris performed a lively Gay Gordons in the drive. They sang and danced and ate and drank until well after midnight.

On Sunday and on Monday, the actual Anniversary itself, Doris and Ernie held 'open house'. There were drinks and wedding cake for all as more than a score of bouquets and literally hundreds of cards filled the house. Steve Massam from BBC Radio Humberside rang in the afternoon and talked to Ernie and Doris live on the programme and two Americans arrived completely out of the blue.

They had been staying in York and saw on a map in a shop the name 'Walkington' - their own surname. They hailed a taxi and told the driver to take them to 'this Walkington place'. When told it was some thirty miles away they didn't bat an eyelid and on arrival went into the village shop whose proprietor quite naturally sent them to see Ernie. They knocked on the door and were surprised to be told by a voice from within to 'come in', Ernie and Doris assuming it was more well-wishers. Only when they saw the cards and flowers did they realise they had walked in on something 'real special'.

1992 is 'real special' as well as the village prepares to celebrate the Silver Jubilee of the Walkington Hayride. As they struggled to harness that pair of horses in the stackyard of Waterworth's farm in 1967 they couldn't possibly have foreseen the outcome of that first comparatively small venture. By 1974 there were six wagons, two Tetley Brewery drays, an icecream float renovated by the Cheesemans of Cottingham, the Rington's Tea float and a variety of gigs and traps from the East Riding Horse and Carriage Club.

By 1986 the single-fold brochure had grown to twenty-eight pages paid for by advertising and sponsorship and with a map of the processional route and a timetable of events. Bilton Grange Old Tyme Music Hall Choir had joined forces with the Hayride songsters and additional entertainment was provided by the Green Ginger Morris Men, Beverley Borough Band, The John Hull Equestrian Display Team and of course Charlie Byass and his Steam Organ. Over forty horse-drawn vehicles were included in the Parade list, nearly half of them being heavy horses. In addition there were several mounted riders and of course Cocky Drew and his penny-farthing.

In 1991 the thirty-two page brochure contained articles by the notable octogenarian horseman and author Herbert Day of Hedon, by Steve Dowler writing about Victorian songs and the weather and by children of Walkington Junior School whose poems and stories gave the view of a new generation. Nearly fifty entrants were listed in the parade, headed by the now traditional Stage Coach 'The Earl of Harewood' driven by Bill Palmer of Cottingham and pulled by four matching chestnut Hungarians.

Despite the appalling weather with unseasonable torrential rain a record amount of thirteen thousand pounds was collected to bring the total donated to charity during the last twenty-four years to over one hundred and eighty-two thousand pounds. Cancer Research has remained the principal beneficiary ever since the first year and will indeed benefit from the sale of this book, but many other charities have been added to the list, both local and national.

Nowadays a variety of supporting events take place during the third week in June - Hayride week. On Wednesday evenings there is a sing-song in the village hall and on Fridays a genuine Barn Dance in the magnificent barn at Northlands Farm, beautifully decorated with fresh-cut bracken, silver streamers and coloured lights. On the Saturday morning a charity stall is manned in Beverley Market stocked with a variety of cakes and goods for sale and in the afternoon there is a Grand Victorian Garden Party in the grounds of the Old Rectory, generously loaned by Mr. and Mrs. Ball. Before the actual Hayride on Sunday morning those who can attend Songs of Praise in All Hallow's Church at 9.30am, many of them already dressed in their beautiful costumes, and even the collection is donated to the Hayride charities.

At 1.30pm on June 21st 1992 the procession proper will start and make its way to Beverley Westwood for the twenty-fifth time. For the twenty-fifth time Ernie will ride on the leading wagon although these days he needs help to mount! For the twenty-fifth time Doris will join the Hayride choir to sing all the old songs, conducted by Ernie in his scarlet tunic - sadly not the one he wore in the Guards which was borrowed by a dramatic society from York and never returned. For the twenty-fifth time collection boxes will be rattled at the many thousands of spectators for whom this has become a very special day.

Long may it and its originator flourish.

# EPILOGUE

Ernie may have had his hey-day but that doesn't mean that he is content to rest on his laurels. He is still very actively involved in village affairs, still Chairman of the Parish Council, still sits on several committees and still keeps tidy the gardens of favourite clients. As I write there are plans in the pipeline for a new village hall, to be built on the site of the old one which has seen such good service and housed so many wonderful events. More plans involve the provision of sheltered accommodation for elderly village residents and in both of these projects Ernie will no doubt play a full part.

To sum up his life of service to the community I talked to Doris and to his daughters, Christine Elston and Pat Rhodes. They all spoke of his single-mindedness when he gets an idea into his head and of how everything else, including his family and especially himself, has often had to take second place. They all agree that money - or the lack of it - has never bothered him. If he could he would do without it altogether.

So how has he rated as husband and father? The word 'devoted' instantly springs to mind. He thinks the world of Doris and has done for over fifty four years. Doris says he has always enjoyed his work, but she worries sometimes that he spends too much time on his committees. Not a 'committee person' herself she puts in more than her fair share of work behind the scenes, but sometimes feels a bit left out at official functions as she doesn't know as many people as Ernie does.

When he first started working for the village he still had a full-time job and Christine remembers him using up his official holidays for his voluntary work so they weren't able to go away on their usual annual holiday all together. Instead Doris would take the girls to stay with her parents. Because of Ernie's dislike of London and his reluctance to let her go on her own she regrets that she never saw as much of her family as she would have liked She has however enjoyed the lovely holidays they have had together since the girls grew up.

As a father both Doris and her daughters agree that Ernie was strict but fair, and always loving. That all embracing love now includes the extended family of sons-in-law and grandchildren. He is proud of what his daughters have achieved and of the way they have followed in his footsteps in service to the community and his grandchildren bring him special joy. One thing that sticks in Doris's mind is bathtime in the Highgate house. Because there was no bathroom the little girls were bathed in front of the fire but woe betide if they made a noise when the football results were on the wireless on a Saturday teatime!

The move to Walkington was popular with both girls. Christine in particular was delighted with the sudden acquisition of a host of new friends in the Collinsons, Taylors and Collingwoods. She also remembers the Coronation celebrations but wasn't aware at the time of her father's involvement. In fact the concept of working for others was something both girls took for granted. They were brought up to be involved, to peel stones of onions for the barbecues, to collect donations, sell raffle tickets and man stalls. Service to the community wasn't an option, it was a part of everyday life.

As the girls grew up decisions about their futures were left very much to them.

There were no pressures for them to go on to higher education and Christine's lifelong ambition to be a nurse was fully backed up when she opted to leave school at sixteen and go as a Nursing Cadet to Beverley Westwood Hospital. She also says that they received a wide education at home For example when she was quite small she could recite the names of every member of the current Cabinet and they were expected to know politics 'inside out'. Pat too left school at sixteen and went into secretarial work which she still enjoys.

Both girls are happily married with families of their own. Pat moved to Hornsea, her husband's home, when she married and has become involved with various charities there. Their daughter Jane is training to be a teacher and son Andrew is still at school.

Christine too moved away on her marriage but only as far as Beverley and even there she missed Walkington so she and husband John have since moved back. They have not only continued to support all the village activities but have set up a fund-raising venture of their own for the Alzheimer's Disease Society. They returned to the village twenty-five years ago just before the birth of their first daughter Julie as they felt that it was a better environment in which to bring up a family. In fact a very pregnant Christine took part in that first Hayride dressed in the concealing smock of a milkmaid. She described it then as 'another of Dad's daft ideas' but now admits that most of the schemes he dreamed up turned into annual events. Julie herself is now married and she in turn has bought a house in the village just down the road from Mum and Dad, while younger sister Lucie is studying Hotel Management in London.

Both Christine and Pat agree that their Mother is wonderful. Despite having gone along with everything their Dad has ever done she has retained her independence of spirit, a trait Christine thinks Doris inherited from her mother. She remembers her Granny Williams as being a very strong character who always worked and had her own money - an unusual thing in her day and age. A shrewd manager, Doris never wastes anything. As children the girls were always almost embarrassingly well dressed as she made all their clothes and they had many new dresses. She has always worked hard both in the home and at various part-time jobs to supplement the familyincome but she has always been there when she was needed.

Christine in particular has cause to be grateful to her as when she decided to complete her education as a mature student Doris looked after the two children full time. Looking back Christine says it must have been very tiring for her Mother as Lucie was only six months old and Julie a wilful toddler and Doris was as strict with them as she had been with her own daughters.

The girls are delighted with the recognition their Father has received in the last few years and recognise that although not well off in monetary terms his wealth is in friendship, job satisfaction and the love of his family. As a married couple Christine says her Mum and Dad are an ideal role model. It has been a marriage of equal partners, each supporting the other, each compensating for the other's strengths weaknesses.

And what of Ernie - how would he sum up his life, past, present and future?

Well there is no doubt that he had enjoyed it and continues to do so. He has several maxims by which he lives including 'Love thy neighbour' which he maintains would solve a lot of the world's problems if it was universally applied. Alan and Florrie

Collingwood have been the Teals' literal neighbours for over forty years to their mutual satisfaction.

Two more quotations Ernie likes are 'Success is to be measured not so much by the position one has reached in life as by the obstacles overcome while trying to succeed' and 'We can do nothing about yesterday but we can do something about tomorrow'. He knows that Walkington's tomorrow will be very different from its yesterday. It has grown and is growing rapidly. It is now more of a dormitory suburb than a country village and its residents are birds of passage rather than families who have lived there for generations, but he is quite sure it will adapt. There is still a very strong community spirit and some 'good young 'uns' willing to take on the time-consuming work of organising the events which have become recognised institutions. He knows it won't be the same and doesn't expect it to be but the ripples of goodwill generated by him and his friends over forty years ago are still spreading.

Towards the end of the war he started thinking about what he would do when he was demobbed. His only real ambition was 'to find a nice spot, get a little house for Doris and the girls and put roses round the door and fill the garden with flowers'. Beyond that, for Ernie, Walkington has been his life. He doesn't ask for more.

And what does Walkington think of Ernie? The following poem, written to commemorate his investiture as President of the Hayride in 1984 says it all.

> For eighteen years you've worked and planned.
> You've given all you had to give.
> You've brought to us in our own land
> A Hayride that will always live.
>
> You told us all we shouldn't worry,
> That on the day the sun would shine.
> You told the horsemen not to hurry.
> 'Just take it slow, you're doing fine'.
>
> And in those years our Hayride's grown,
> The fame of Walkington has spread.
> The whole idea was yours alone.
> 'It'll be great' you always said.
>
> And great it is - and greater yet
> With you to guide it will become,
> For Walkington will not forget
> The man who beat a lonely drum.
>
> For all the courage, all the fears,
> For all the battles lost and won,
> For all the Hayrides down the years
> We thank you Ernie for the fun.
>
> So let us greet out man of laughter,
> Fill your glass, let church bells peal.
> From Walkington now and hereafter
> The toast is always 'ERNIE TEAL!'